TELL ME ABOUT SCIENCE

An Hachette UK Company
www.hachette.co.uk

First published in Great Britain in 2016 by Chancellor Press,
a division of Octopus Publishing Group Ltd
Carmelite House, 50 Victoria Embankment, London EC4Y 0DZ
www.octopusbooks.co.uk

Edited and designed by Anna Southgate and Leah Germann

ISBN 978-0-7537-3030-0

A CIP catalogue record for this book is available from the British Library

Printed and bound in China

10 9 8 7 6 5 4 3 2 1

Publisher: Lucy Pessell
Design Manager: Megan van Staden
Editor: Natalie Bradley
Production Controller: Sarah Kulasek-Boyd

UPDATED & REVISED

TELL ME ABOUT SCIENCE

ANSWERS TO HUNDREDS OF FASCINATING QUESTIONS

CHANCELLOR PRESS

CONTENTS

PLANET EARTH

CONTENTS

WHEN WAS THE EARTH FORMED?

Some 225 million years ago all the world's landmasses were joined together into one supercontinent, the Pangaea, surrounded by a single universal sea, the Panthalassa.

No one knows for certain when the Earth was formed. However, scientists have reasoned that it probably formed around 6,000 million years ago. This figure is twice as long as when the first signs of life are believed to have appeared on Earth, about 3,000 million years ago. The most scientific reasoning for the creation of Earth is that it began as a huge ball of hot gases, which cooled to form the planet. Seas of dissolved chemicals would have covered the land, and the air would have been an atmosphere of different gases. The atmosphere was thought to have consisted of swirling gaseous clouds, which most likely caused huge electrical storms. The poisonous gases in the atmosphere must have reacted to produce oxygen, which triggered off the first beginnings of life on Earth.

• FACT FILE •

As Earth cooled down, it gave off clouds of steam and gas. The moisture in these clouds eventually turned to rain, which formed the first seas.

OF HOW MANY PARTS DOES THE EARTH CONSIST?

The Earth consists of five parts: the first, the atmosphere, is gaseous; the second, the hydrosphere, is liquid; the third, fourth and fifth, the lithosphere, mantle and core, are largely solid. The atmosphere is the gaseous envelope that surrounds the solid body of the planet. Although it has a thickness of more than 1,100km (700 miles), about half its mass is concentrated in the lower 5.6km (3.5 miles). The lithosphere, consisting mainly of the cold, rigid, rocky crust of the Earth, extends to a depth of 100km (60 miles). The hydrosphere is the layer of water that, in the form of the oceans, covers roughly 70 per cent of the surface of the Earth. The mantle and core are the heavy interior of the Earth, making up most of the Earth's mass.

• FACT FILE •

The Earth's inner core is made up mostly of iron and nickel. It is 1,370km (850 miles) deep and is thought to have a temperature of around 4,500°C (8,132°F).

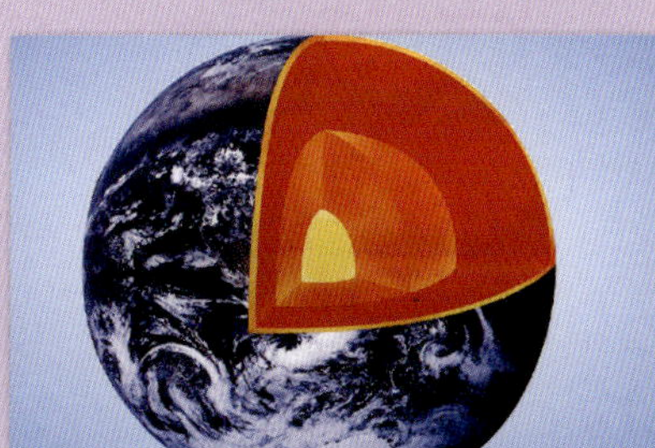

WHAT DEFINES A DAY?

For early peoples, the only changes that were truly regular, were the motions of objects in the sky. The most obvious of these changes was the alternate daylight and darkness, caused by the rising and setting of the Sun. Each of these cycles of the Sun came to be called a day. Another regular change in the sky was the change in the visible shape of the Moon. Each cycle of the Moon's changing shape takes about 29½ days, or a month. The cycle of the seasons gave people an even longer unit of time. The seven-day week came from the Jewish custom of observing a Sabbath (day of rest) every seventh day.

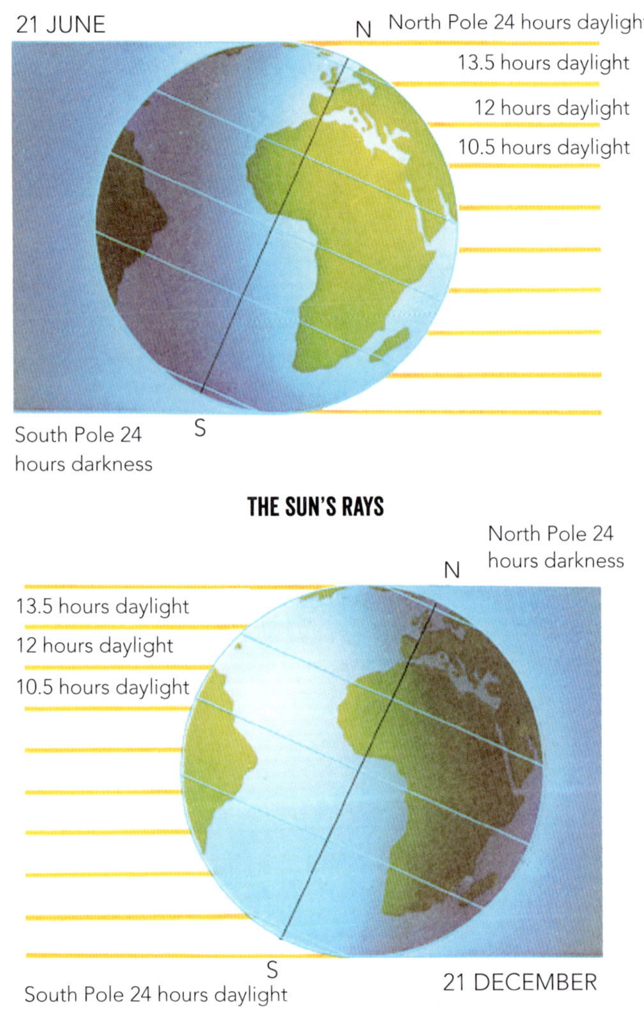

• FACT FILE •

Some clock faces are divided into 24 hours. On such a clock, 9 a.m. would be shown as 09:00 and 4 p.m. would be 16:00. This system avoids confusion between the morning and evening hours.

? **DID YOU KNOW THAT THE DIVISION OF A DAY INTO 24 HOURS, AN HOUR INTO 60 MINUTES, AND A MINUTE INTO 60 SECONDS PROBABLY CAME FROM THE ANCIENT BABYLONIANS?**

WHAT IS A HEMISPHERE?

The Equator is an imaginary line drawn around the outside of the Earth. It divides the Earth into two halves, called hemispheres.

Hemisphere is the name given to any half of the globe. It comes from a Greek word that means 'half a sphere'.

Geographers divide the Earth into hemispheres by using the Equator as a boundary line. All areas north of the Equator make up the Northern Hemisphere. All areas to the south make up the Southern Hemisphere.

The Earth may also be divided into a land hemisphere and a water hemisphere. The land hemisphere includes the half of the Earth with the most land. Its middle lies near London, England. The other half of the Earth, Mostly water, makes up the water hemisphere. Its middle lies near New Zealand.

• FACT FILE •

Mapmakers puzzled for many years how to draw the curved surface of the globe accurately onto a sheet of paper. In 1569, Gerardus Mercator showed how to convert the rounded shape of the world into a cylindrical shape. By dividing the Earth into 'orange peel' segments it gave a truer image of the size of the countries.

HOW DOES GRAVITY WORK?

Gravity is the force that pulls towards the centre of the Earth. It doesn't matter where you stand on the Earth's surface, the ground is always 'down'. The force of gravity depends on the mass, or amount of material, of an object. Objects only feel heavy because of their mass.

Newton realized that gravity not only affects the Earth, but it also controls the movement of the planets and the stars, as well as the orbit of the Moon around the Earth. When you whirl something around your head on the end of a piece of string it flies outwards and appears to defy the force of gravity. This is called centrifugal force. When you let go of the string the centrifugal force makes the object fly off in a straight line.

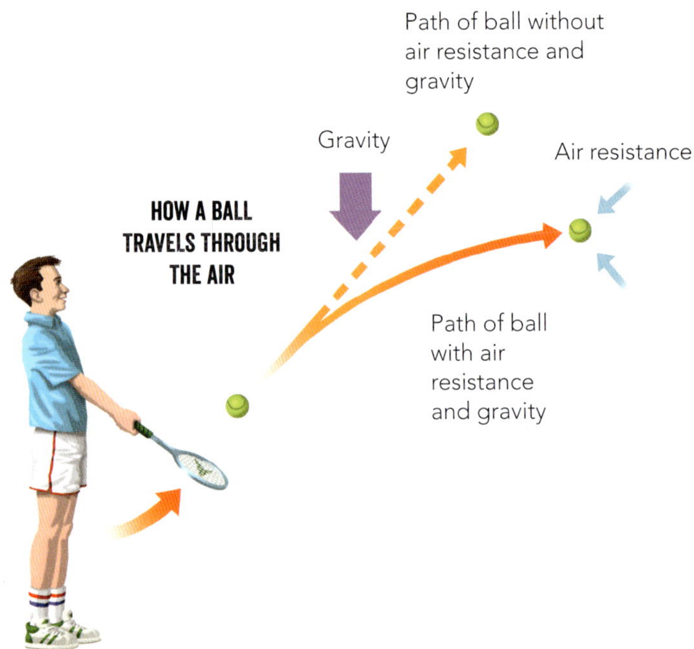

FACT FILE

Sir Isaac Newton (1643–1727) was the first scientist to develop the laws of gravity. He supposedly was inspired by seeing an apple fall from a tree.

WHAT IS THE WEIGHT OF THE ATMOSPHERE?

IF THE ATMOSPHERE COULD SOMEHOW BE COMPRESSED AND PUT ON A SET OF SCALES, IT WOULD WEIGH ABOUT 5,170 QUADRILLION TONNES!

The Earth is surrounded by a thick blanket of air. This is its atmosphere. The Earth's atmosphere is made up of about 20 different gases. The two main ones are oxygen and nitrogen. It also contains water and dust particles. Air is matter, and like all matter it has weight. Weight is the measure of the pull of gravity on matter. If a scale registers ten pounds when a stone is placed on it, this means that gravity is pulling the stone with a force of ten pounds. Similarly, Earth's gravity pulls on each particle of gas and dust in the atmosphere. Because our atmosphere is a vast ocean of air, it has considerable weight. The Earth's atmosphere is one of the things that makes it a planet of life.

• FACT FILE •

Our knowledge of air pressure has enabled us to understand the physics behind aircraft flight. Air passing over the top of a plane's wings reduces in pressure, allowing higher pressure under the wings to exert an upward force, so the plane can fly.

WHEN ARE MOUNTAINS FORMED?

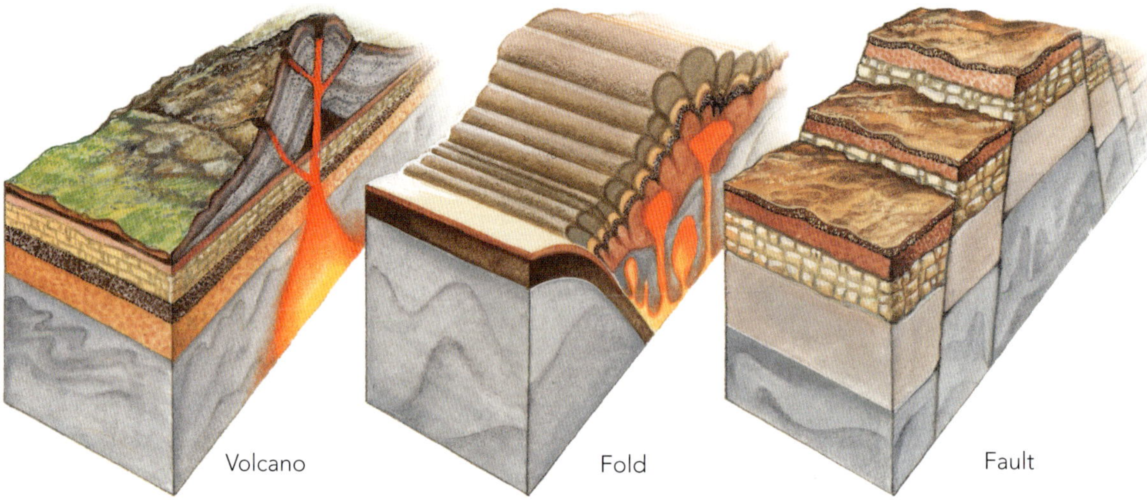

Faults in the rocks normally occur when there is a lot of pressure on the rocks. Mountain building is a slow process and happens over centuries.

Mountains can be formed in three different ways. Volcanoes form mountains when lava from deep inside the Earth cools and hardens on the surface. Other mountains are formed when two plates move towards each other under pressure or where an oceanic plate is pushed under a continental crust. The pressure causes the ground near the joining plate margins to fault and fold. The ground is forced upwards to form mountains. The Rockies, Alps, Andes, Urals and Himalayas were all formed in this way. Finally the Earth's crust can fracture and create faults which means that large blocks of land can be moved upwards or downwards.

• FACT FILE •

Rockslides are common where forests have been destroyed on mountainsides. There are no longer any tree roots to stabilize the loose material.

WHERE DID THE FIRST FORESTS DEVELOP?

The first forests on Earth developed in the Devonian Period, between 416 and 359 million years ago in swampy ground near the coasts. The first forests were quite low-growing and consisted of ferns and similar plants, but these evolved rapidly and grew quite tall. Fossils of Archaeopteris – tree-like ferns that date from the late Devonian – have been found in Europe, Morocco, North America and Australia. They are related to the tree ferns that are found today in Australia, Malaysia and New Zealand. At the end of the Devonian, trees almost 30m (100ft) tall were not uncommon and the first seed-bearing plants had evolved. Such trees form the oldest coal seams on Earth.

?

DID YOU KNOW THAT THE TAIGA IS THE LARGEST HABITAT ON PLANET EARTH? IT IS MAINLY FOREST LAND THAT STRETCHES ACROSS NORTHERN USA AND CANADA, SOUTHERN ICELAND, NORWAY, FINLAND AND SWEDEN, THEN THROUGH RUSSIA, KAZAKHSTAN, MONGOLIA AND NORTHERN JAPAN.

• FACT FILE •

As plants colonized the land during the Devonian Period, animals were not far behind. Marine animals adapted to life on land and scorpions, mites, centipedes, spiders and early amphibians are known to have existed at this time.

WHEN DO EARTHQUAKES OCCUR?

Our planet is a very restless place. Every 30 seconds, the ground suddenly rumbles and trembles. Most of the movements are so slight that they are not felt. Others can be so large that they cause complete disaster. Big cracks appear in the land, streets buckle and buildings simply crumble. In fact whole towns and cities can be destroyed. These are called earthquakes and the reason they occur is because the Earth's crust is made up of moving parts called plates. When these plates slide past or into each other, the rocks jolt and send out shock waves.

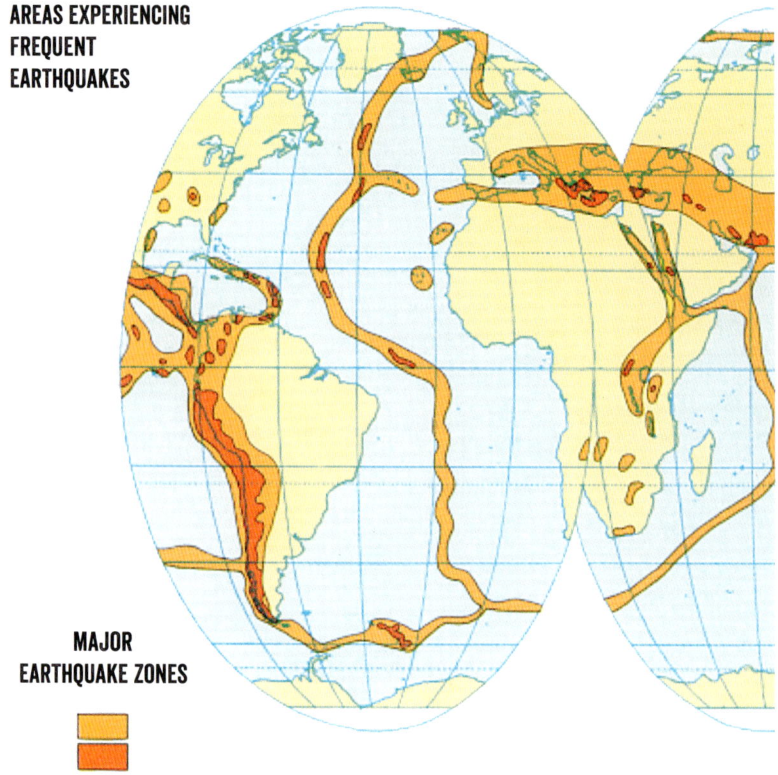

• FACT FILE •

Both mining and tunnelling operations are known to have caused earthquakes in areas that are already under tension due to movements in the Earth's crust.

WHEN DO WE USE A SEISMOGRAPH?

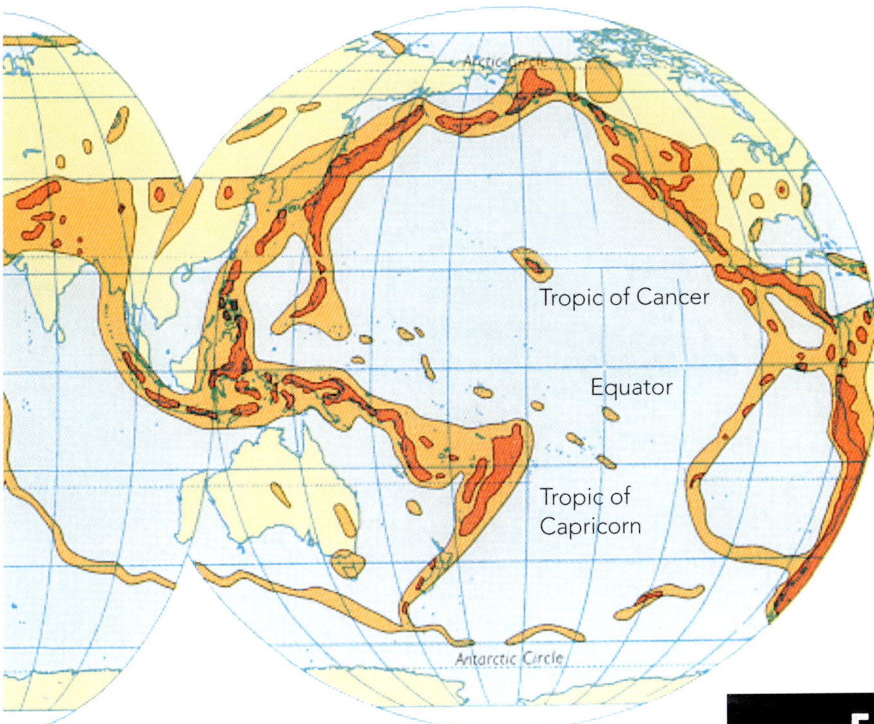

?

DID YOU KNOW THAT THE LARGEST RECORDED EARTHQUAKE REACHED A MAGNITUDE 9.5? IT HAPPENED IN CHILE IN 1960.

Sometimes there is a big news story about an earthquake that happened in some distant part of the world. Although you didn't feel the Earth shake, scientists probably made a complete and exact record of that earthquake. They have special instruments called seismographs. The study of earthquakes is called seismology. The seismograph picks up the vibrations that are caused by one rock mass rubbing against the other. The energy of this rubbing is changed to vibration in the rocks. This vibration can travel many thousands of miles.

• FACT FILE •

The edges of the Pacific plate are surrounded by earthquakes, volcanic activity and hot springs, caused by the crust shifts and hot lava rises near the surface.

WHEN DO MONSOONS OCCUR?

A monsoon is a season of very heavy rain falling in tropical countries. Monsoons are most common near the Equator. They occur when seasonal winds spring up carrying moist air in from the sea. Important crops such as rice depend entirely on the monsoon season to provide the right growing conditions.

If the monsoon rains fail, famine commonly follows. There are also some special winds called monsoon winds. These are winds that change their direction with the season. In India, the monsoons blow south as hot, dry winds in the wintertime, and blow north in the summer, bringing heavy rainfall.

CHERRAPUNJI, IN INDIA IS THE WETTEST PLACE ON EARTH. ON 15–16 JUNE 1995, THE CITY HAD 2,493MM (98IN) OF RAIN IN JUST 48 HOURS!

FACT FILE

The Aborigines believe that if a possum is left cooking by the water's edge, a sizzling sound is produced. This noise irritates the rainbow snake, who they believe crawls underground towards the source of the noise. As it moves along, the weather turns stormy, and the monsoon rains begin.

WHEN DOES WATER BECOME SALTY?

Water becomes salty when minerals (including salts) dissolve into it. This process begins when rainwater falls on the land and erodes rock. The minerals found in rock are dissolved into the rainwater. These dissolved minerals in the rainwater enter streams and rivers, gradually working their way into the seas and oceans.

This is a process that is constantly taking place in the sea, so the level and concentration of salt in the oceans and seas is always increasing. Some of the minerals are consumed by organisms in the water, but the vast majority of them constitute the saltiness of the water.

• FACT FILE •

Lighthouses were built to warn ships at sea that they were approaching land and rocky water. Their beam of light across the waves made travelling by boat much safer.

WHEN DO WE SEE MIRAGES?

Mirages form in hot deserts where the air is so hot it bends and distorts light rays. The shimmering images that a mirage produces have often tricked travellers in deserts. People think that they can see an oasis or town on the horizon, but in reality it is not there.

Under certain conditions, such as a stretch of pavement or desert air heated by intense sunshine, the air rapidly cools with elevation and therefore increases in density and refractive power. Sunlight reflected downward from the top of an object, for example the camel above, will be directed through the cool air in the normal way. When the sky is the object of the mirage, the land is mistaken for a lake or sheet of water.

• FACT FILE •

About one-third of the world's land surface is covered by desert. Deserts are found wherever there is too little water to allow much plant life to grow. Salt deserts form when shallow seas and lakes dry up, leaving a deposit of smooth salt.

WHEN ARE DESERTS COLD?

About one-third of the world's land surface is covered by desert. Not all these deserts are hot and arid.

Antarctica is the biggest cold desert in the world. The blanket of two-km-thick ice covering the Tundra, howling winds and freezing temperatures stop plants and land-living animals from surviving. But the ocean around this frozen desert is full of fish and krill, so the coasts are home to millions of birds. Once the Antarctic winter sun sets, it is dark for more than two months.

The Gobi desert in Mongolia and western China is also very cold in the winter, when temperatures drop below freezing. However, the temperature in the summer is hot.

Among the animals that live in the Tundra are grizzly bears, white wolves, lemmings, shrews, caribou and grey falcons.

• FACT FILE •

One of the animals that has survived the Arctic conditions is the polar bear. In very cold climates, animals need excellent insulation to stop their body heat from escaping. This can be in the form of dense hair, fur or feathers, or on the inside, in the form of a thick layer of fat or blubber.

WHEN DOES A LUNAR ECLIPSE OCCUR?

LUNAR ECLIPSE

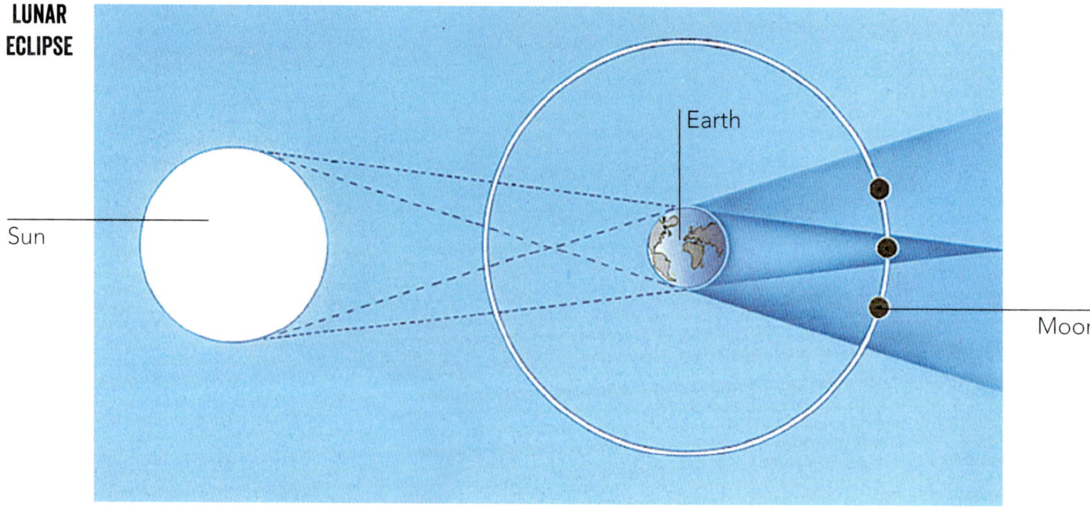

The Earth casts a long shadow into space, and when this shadow passes over the Moon it can cause an eclipse.

A lunar eclipse can only happen during a full Moon, when the Sun is directly behind the Earth. It happens only occasionally, because the orbit of the Moon is slightly tilted and so the shadow usually misses it. Lunar eclipses can last for over one hour, but they do not completely black out the shadowed part of the Moon. Some sunlight filters through, making the shadow look a reddish-brown colour. Eclipses can only be seen from certain parts of the world.

• FACT FILE •

The distance of the Moon from the Earth was settled when the Apollo astronauts left a small reflector on the Moon's surface. This distance is 384,000 km (238,606 miles), though it varies slightly because the Moon does not have a perfectly circular orbit.

WHEN DOES A SOLAR ECLIPSE OCCUR?

SOLAR ECLIPSE

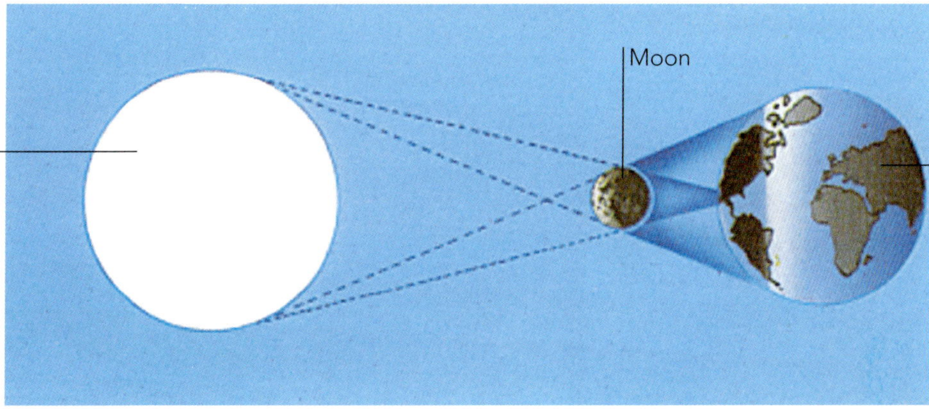

The Moon is 400 times smaller than the Sun but about 400 times closer. So we see them both as being about the same size.

A solar eclipse is when the Moon blocks out the light from the Sun. This can make the day turn dark as all the light from the Sun is blocked out in a total eclipse. In a partial eclipse only part of the light is blocked out.

The Sun is our nearest star. It is 149.6 million km (92.9 million miles) away from Earth. It is the heat and light from the Sun that makes life on Earth possible. The huge gravity pull of the Sun keeps the planets of our Solar System orbiting around it.

? **DID YOU KNOW THAT YOU CAN DAMAGE YOUR RETINA BY WATCHING A SOLAR ECLIPSE WITHOUT SOME SORT OF PROTECTION FOR YOUR EYES?**

• FACT FILE •

The daily rise and fall of the ocean's tides occur because of the pull from the Moon and the Sun. There is a smaller pull from the Sun. When the Moon and Sun are in line there are high spring tides.

WHEN DOES THE SUN STOP SHINING?

The Sun is our nearest star. Stars are massive nuclear reactors generating energy in their cores. It is the heat and light from the Sun that makes life on Earth possible. The Sun for us is a pretty steady and dependable thing. Whether we can see it or not, we know it is always there, and the answer to this question is – the Sun NEVER stops shining.

As the Earth spins on its axis, the Sun always shines on one side giving us daylight. Another time when the Sun is not visible is during a solar eclipse. This is when the Moon blocks the Sun's light from the Earth, so that the Sun seems to disappear.

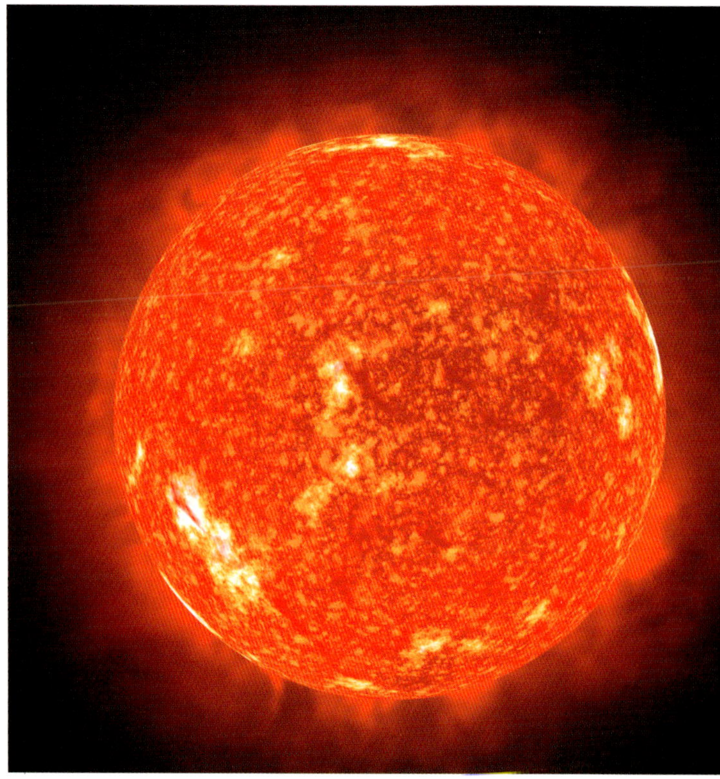

• FACT FILE •

The direction of the Earth's rotation means that the Sun appears to rise in the east and set in the west. The Earth rotates towards the east, so the Sun first becomes visible from that direction.

WHEN DO WE SEE THE SPECTRUM OF LIGHT?

Rainbows happen when light passes through raindrops and is reflected and refracted by the shape of the droplets.

Sir Isaac Newton of Cambridge University first uncovered the secrets of how light is divided up. We think of ordinary light as being 'white', but really light is a mixture of red, orange, yellow, green, blue and violet. When sunlight strikes the bevelled edge of a mirror, or the edge of a glass prism, or the surface of a soap bubble, we can see the different hues in light. What actually happens is that the white light is broken up into the different wavelengths that are seen by our eyes. These wavelengths form a band of parallel stripes, each hue grading into the one next to it. This band is called a 'spectrum'. In a spectrum the red line is always at one end and the blue and violet lines at the other.

• FACT FILE •

Sir Isaac Newton used his discoveries about light to build a new kind of telescope. It used a reflecting mirror instead of glass lenses to magnify images.

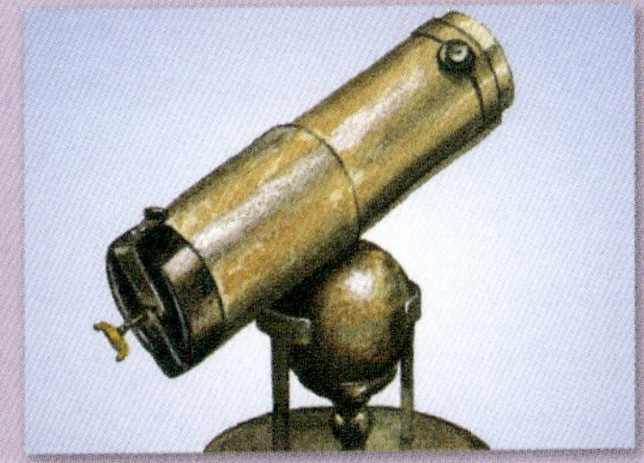

WHEN DOES PHOTOSYNTHESIS OCCUR?

Photosynthesis is the process by which green plants and certain other organisms transform light energy into chemical energy. During photosynthesis in green plants, light energy is captured and used to convert water, carbon dioxide, and minerals into oxygen and energy-rich organic compounds. The plant contains packets of a green pigment called chlorophyll, which carry out this process. During photosynthesis water and carbon dioxide from the air are converted into sugars that nourish the plant. The plant releases oxygen into the air at the same time.

• FACT FILE •

The process of photosynthesis takes place mostly in the leaves of a plant. Leaves are large and flattened so that a large area is exposed to sunlight.

WHEN DO ANIMALS HIBERNATE?

Hibernating animals include bats, skunks, squirrels, hedgehogs and bees.

The word 'hibernate' comes from Latin and means 'winter sleep'. Certain animals hibernate during the winter months to escape the severe weather conditions and because food is hard to find. The sleep of a true hibernator, like the hedgehog, is quite unlike ordinary sleep. The temperature of its body decreases until it is only a little warmer than the air of its den. Because of this, the animal burns the food stored in their bodies very, very slowly. They need less oxygen, and as a result their breathing is slower and their hearts beat only faintly. When spring comes, the animals are awakened by the change in temperature, moisture, and by hunger.

• FACT FILE •

Many mammals, like the bear, do not really hibernate. They do sleep more in the winter than in the summer, but it is not the deep sleep of hibernation.

WHAT IS A PECKING ORDER?

A living animal behaves constantly in order to survive, and all animals must solve the same basic problems. Animals do whatever they can to acquire all the energy they can use, and in this basic sense each is competing with all the others. Among animals that live in groups, one becomes the clear leader. In chickens, this means that one bird dominates all of the other birds.

The next one down in the 'pecking order' can dominate all except the leader, and so on, until the bird at the bottom of this process can be bullied by the entire flock. This can also be seen in families with dogs. The dog remains at the bottom of the pecking order and submits to the human members of the family.

• FACT FILE •

Dog fights do not usually cause too much damage. The loser will usually submit by lying down, which reduces the level of aggression in the dominant dog.

WHAT IS THE FOOD CHAIN?

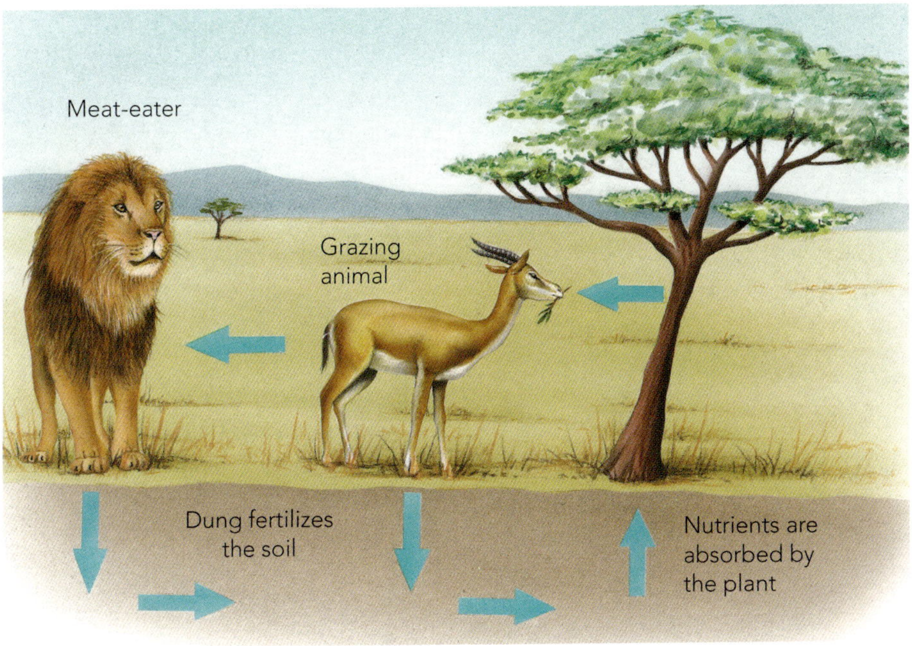

A food chain is a sequence that demonstrates how one organism forms the food for another. It begins with the simplest animals and plants, and continues until the top of the chain is reached. Humans or predator animals are often at the top of food chains.

Plants such as grass and trees are towards the bottom of a food chain. Grazing animals browse on these plants, and these animals are in turn eaten by predators such as lions. Their dung fertilizes the soil, encouraging the growth of more plants, so the food chain actually becomes a complete circle.

• FACT FILE •

In overpopulated areas, people commonly increase the total food supply by cutting out one step in the food chain: instead of consuming animals that eat cereal grains, the people themselves consume the grains.

WHY DO LIVING THINGS HAVE LATIN NAMES?

Latin names for living things include *Bellis perennis* (common daisy), *Malaclemys terrapin* (diamondback terrapin) and *Galeocerdo cuvier* (tiger shark).

Most plants and animals have local, popular names, but a system needed to be devised so that they were recognized everywhere. Carl Linnaeus (1707–1778), a brilliant scientist, established the modern scientific method of 'binomial nomenclature' or two names, in which the first word was used to describe the genus and the second the distinguishing characteristic of a specific living thing, and perhaps the inclusion of the name of the person who discovered it. At the time of Linnaeus' work, Latin, the language of science, was taught everywhere and was uniquely suitable for this system of naming plants and animals.

• FACT FILE •

The Latin name for a human is *Homo sapiens*, meaning 'thinking man'. A fossil form of Homo, or man, is *Homo habillis* (tool-using man).

WHY IS CHARLES DARWIN REMEMBERED?

The English naturalist Charles Darwin, is remembered chiefly for his work, *On the Origin of Species*, in which he established, after many years of study and voyages of exploration, that all species have descended, over time, from common ancestors. He also formed the scientific theory that this 'evolution' was the result of a process of 'natural selection' of the characteristics that would guarantee survival most successfully in specific environments. He noted this phenomenon particularly in the unique Galapagos Islands.

• FACT FILE •

The giraffe is an example of how natural selection helps evolution. Their ancestors had longer than average necks so that they could reach more food.

The giant tortoise is just one of the animals that Charles Darwin discovered when he visited the Galapagos Islands.

WHICH PROCESS REUSES EVERYDAY WASTE?

Recycling is the process that resuses everyday waste, such as cans, glass containers, newspapers and office paper. The process is designed to collect, process and reuse materials instead of throwing them away. Recycling programmes also collect plastics and used motor oil. Recycling helps conserve raw materials and energy that manufacturers would otherwise use to make new products. Recycling keeps materials out of landfills (areas where wastes are deposited and covered with earth or other material), saving scarce landfill space. Recycling also helps reduce the pollution that may result from waste disposal.

• FACT FILE •

When you buy a new car it may not be quite as new as you think. Up to 40% of the steel may have come from old cars. Recycling scrap steel saves raw materials and energy.

THERE IS AT LEAST 20 TIMES MORE PLASTIC PRODUCED TODAY THAN THERE WAS 50 YEARS AGO!

HOW CAN AEROSOLS DAMAGE THE EARTH?

Scientists have discovered a gap in the protective ozone layer around the Earth. Ozone, a form of oxygen, filters out more than 90 per cent of the Sun's harmful rays. The hole in the ozone layer has been blamed on our use of chemicals called chlorofluorocarbons (or CFCs). They were widely used in refrigerators, freezers and aerosol cans. The use of CFCs has now been heavily restricted for several yeats, and some reports suggest that the ozone layer is now repairing itself.

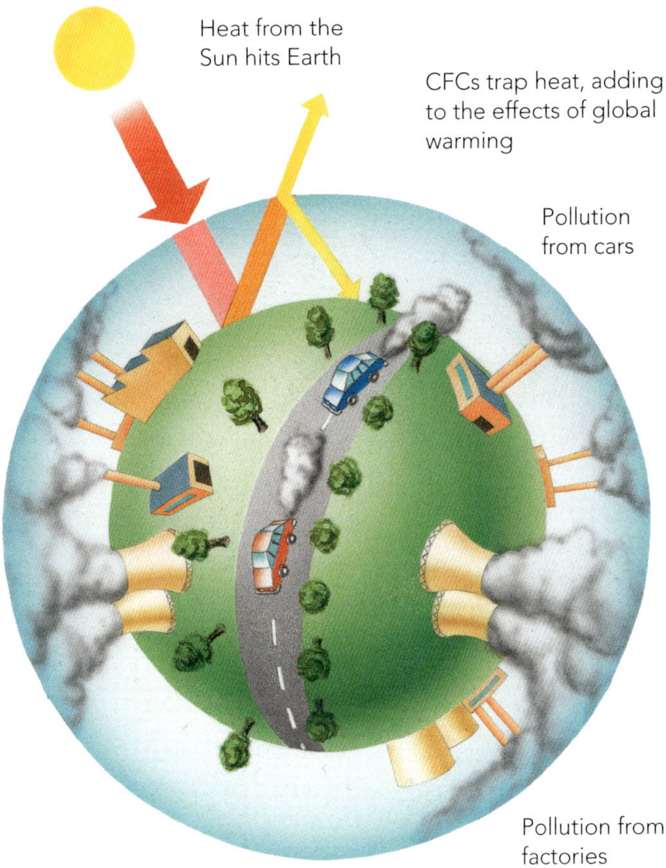

• FACT FILE •

Mammoths lived in an area with a cool climate, but gradually the weather began to get warmer. Unable to adapt, the mammoth became extinct.

IN THE LABORATORY

CONTENTS

WHY DO SCIENTISTS WEAR PROTECTIVE CLOTHING?

Two of the many things that scientists study are germs and bacteria that carry diseases. As many of these could be extremely dangerous if touched, or sometimes just breathed in, it is essential for the scientist to wear protective clothing that includes masks, gloves, body and head protection.

Scientists sometimes have to handle radioactive material. Exposure to radioactive radiation can be fatal to any living organism. For this reason robots are used rather than human beings if at all possible. When people do need to handle such substances they wear protective clothing and carry a meter that records the amount of exposure to radiation they are receiving.

• FACT FILE •

This symbol on a container or building warns that there is some radioactive material inside.

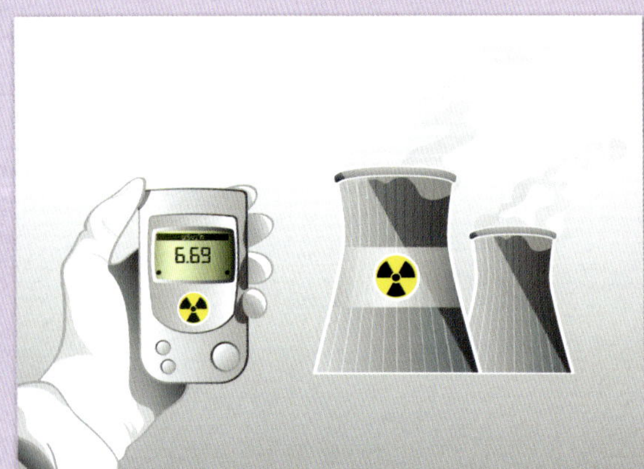

DID YOU KNOW THAT THE RADIOACTIVE CHEMICAL ELEMENT PLUTONIUM IS ONE OF THE MOST DANGEROUS SUBSTANCES IN THE WORLD?

WHERE WOULD YOU USE A BUNSEN BURNER?

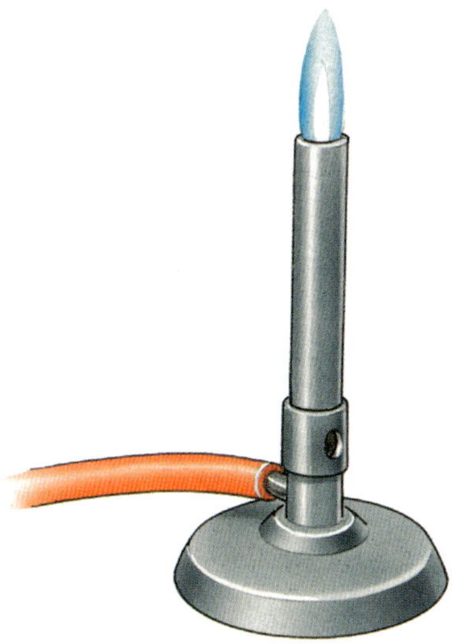

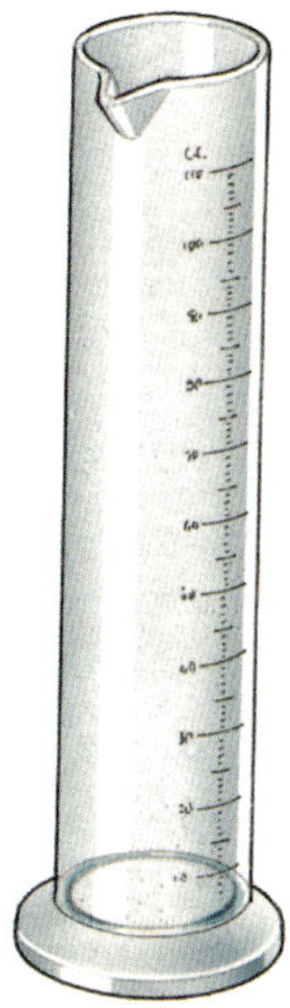

Scientists sometimes use Bunsen burners to heat tools in order to sterilize them prior to use, or to speed up a chemical reaction.

A Bunsen burner is a gas burner used for heating substances in scientific laboratories. It consists of a metal tube on a stand and a long rubber hose that connects the tube to a gas jet. Several adjustable openings at the bottom of the tube control the amount of air that enters and mixes with the gas. The temperature of the flame is regulated by increasing or decreasing the amount of air in the tube. Because the gas mixes with air before burning, it produces a smokeless flame.

• FACT FILE •

The Bunsen burner was invented in the 1850s by a German chemist called Robert William Bunsen. He became famous for his work in using a spectrometer to identify chemical elements.

WHY ARE ATOMS EVERYWHERE?

Atoms are the tiny particles that make up the whole Universe. Enormous amounts of energy are locked inside atoms. Atoms are the tiniest particles into which a substance can be divided without changing into something else. Atoms actually consist almost entirely of open space, in which tiny particles orbit the central particle, or nucleus. The particles travel so fast that they seem to be solid. Atoms are so minute that the smallest particle visible to the naked eye would contain about one million billion atoms. Despite their tiny size, atoms can be seen individually under very powerful electron microscopes.

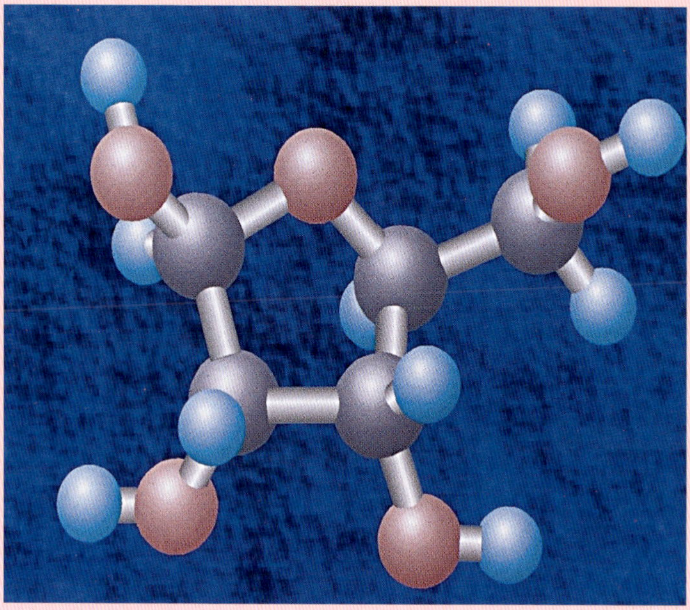

There are more than 109 different atoms. Atoms are so incredibly tiny – about 100,000 million atoms fit on this full stop •

• FACT FILE •

An atom becomes linked to other atoms by electrical bonds, which work rather like chemical hooks. Some atoms only carry one of these hooks, while others may have many. Atoms with many hooks can build up with other atoms into complicated molecules or chemical compounds.

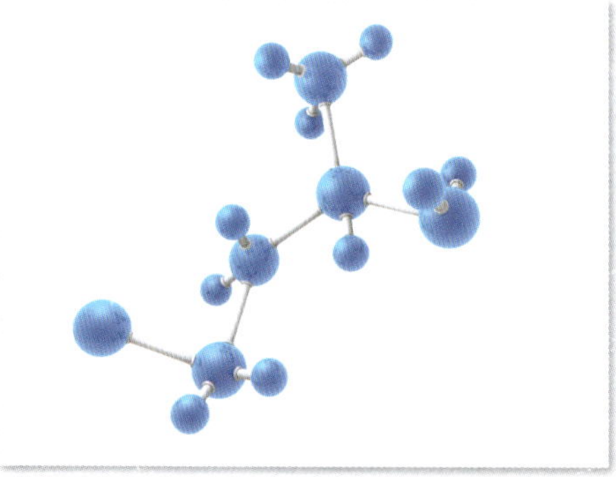

WHEN DID RUTHERFORD FIRST SPLIT THE ATOM?

Ernest Rutherford (1871–1937) was a physicist who studied radioactivity. He found several different forms of radiation and also discovered that elements change as a result of radioactive decay. He received the Nobel Prize for his work. Rutherford went on to discover the nucleus of the atom, and in 1919 he finally succeeded in splitting an atom for the first time.

He described the atom as a tiny, dense, positively charged core called a nucleus, in which nearly all the mass is concentrated, around which the light, negative constituents, called electrons, circulate at some distance, much like planets revolving around the Sun.

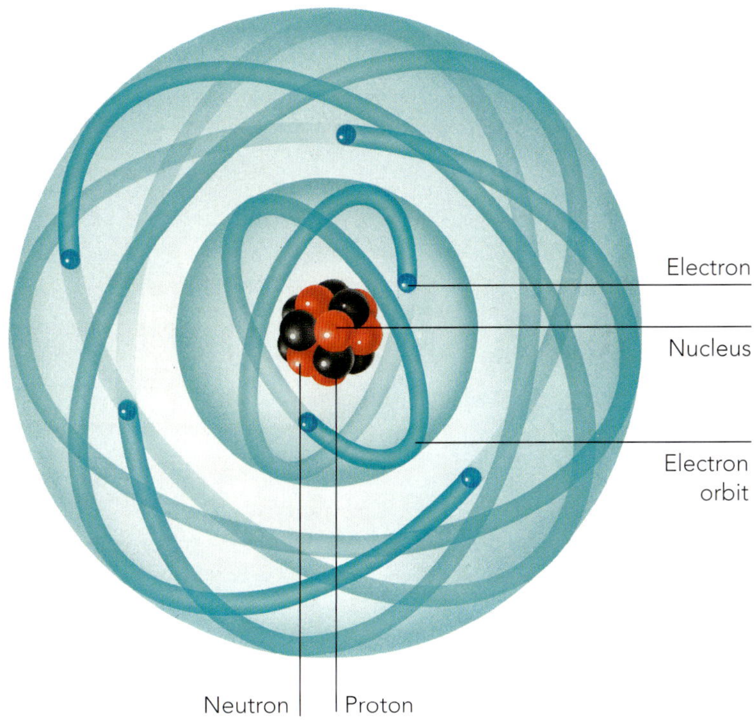

• FACT FILE •

Quantum physics helps us to understand how energy is used or released by atoms. Negatively charged electrons circle about the positively charged nucleus of the atom. They stay in the same orbit until this is disturbed, and each orbit has its own level of energy.

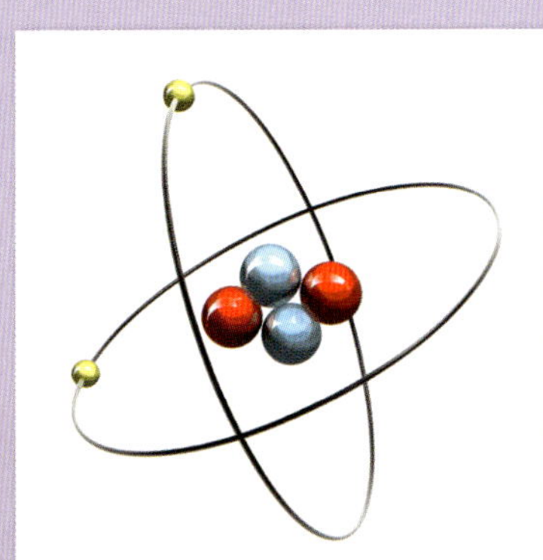

HOW IS PENICILLIN MADE?

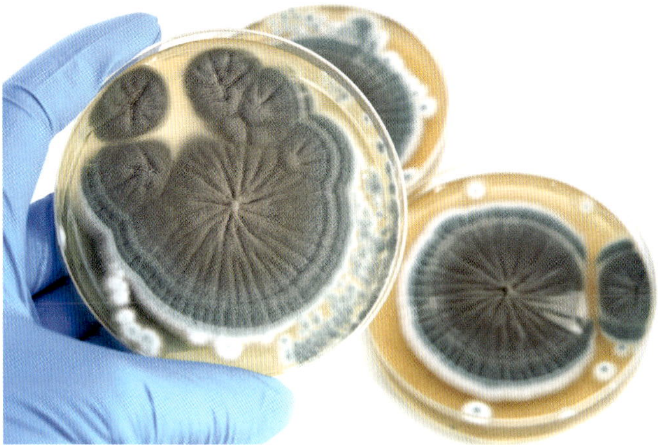

The story goes that Fleming left his lab in a bit of a mess when he went on holiday and it was on his return that he discovered he had cultivated penicillin fungi.

Penicillin is one of nature's own miracles. It is the name we give to a powerful substance that fights bacteria and which is developed by certain moulds. It is an 'antibiotic', which means it is a substance produced by a living organism and acts upon other harmful organisms or bacteria.

Penicillin was discovered almost by accident, in 1928, by Sir Alexander Fleming, but it soon became the subject of intensive study. It was found that certain moulds produced this substance that had a powerful and destructive effect on many of the common bacteria that infect man, while it had no effect on many others.

Penicillin is very selective, so other antibiotics have been developed by scientists to fight other harmful bacteria. It can also be manufactured artificially for mass production.

• FACT FILE •

In 1347 a dreadful plague spread throughout London. Known as the 'Black Death', this epidemic was caused by rats. The disease was very infectious, and so spread rapidly, causing many thousands of deaths.

HOW DO BACTERIA AND VIRUSES DIFFER?

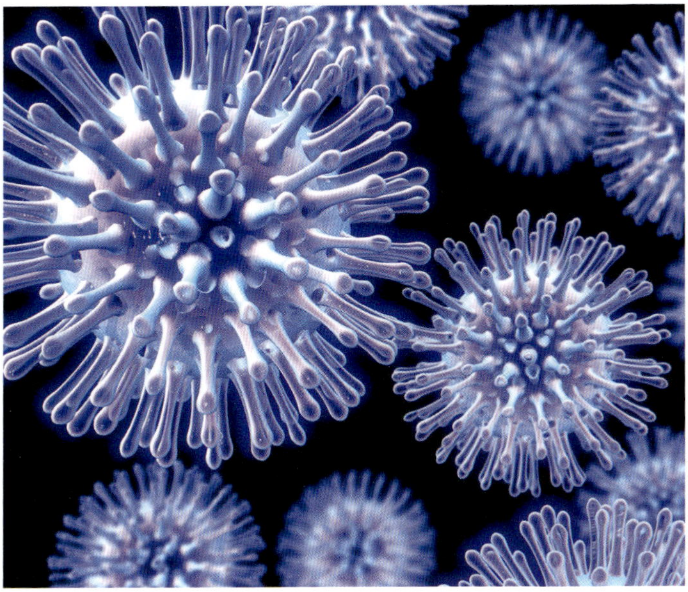
Virus

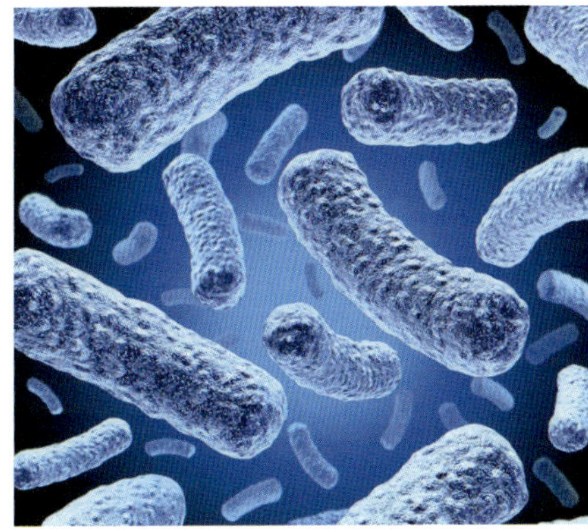
Bacteria

Bacteria are the simplest true living organism. Unlike other living cells, bacteria do not have a nucleus – their genes are scattered throughout their interior. Bacteria have a thick protective cell wall. There are thousands of bacteria in every single cubic metre of air that you breathe. Everything you touch is loaded with bacteria. They even live inside your body. Although bacteria can cause disease, the majority of them are completely harmless. They carry out the vital function of breaking down dead and waste materials. Bacteria in your gut, for example, help the body to digest food.

Viruses are even smaller than bacteria, but strictly speaking are not alive. To be 'alive' an organism must be able to grow and reproduce. Viruses cannot do this themselves and the only way they can reproduce is to enter a living cell and take control of it. This cell then becomes a living factory that can produce more viruses.

• FACT FILE •

Scientists are always looking for new cures for illnesses and diseases. Rainforests contain the bulk of the world's species of plants and trees. Each year new plants are discovered, and valuable plant chemicals are found. Hopefully one day these will become a valuable source of medicine.

WHO DEVELOPED VACCINATION?

British doctor, Edward Jenner (1749–1823) made the initial developments in vaccination. He was born in the village of Berkeley, in England, and trained as a surgeon before studying medicine in London. He returned home as a doctor in 1773. Jenner became interested in milkmaid Sarah Nelmes, who boasted that she could not catch smallpox because she had earlier caught the less serious disease cowpox from the cows she milked. A smallpox outbreak in 1788 proved that she was right. None of Jenner's patients who had caught cowpox got smallpox. In 1796, Jenner proved his theory by infecting a small boy first with cowpox and then with smallpox. He found that the boy was immune to the disease.

• FACT FILE •

Jenner called his treatment vaccination (from the Latin word for cowpox – *vaccina*).

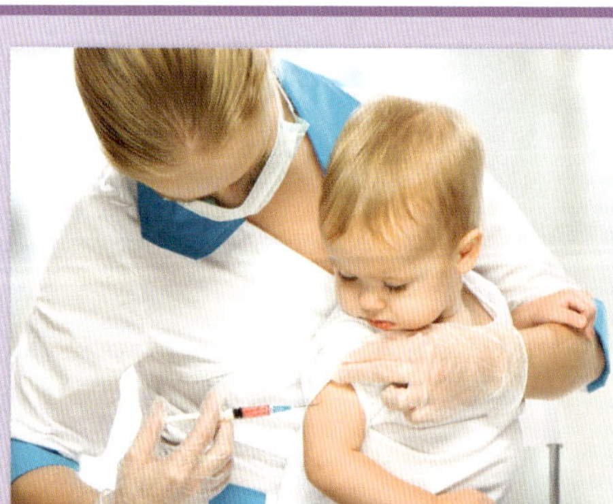

?

DID YOU KNOW THAT, THANKS TO VACCINATION, SMALLPOX WAS THE FIRST DISEASE EVER TO BE TOTALLY ERADICATED FROM THE WORLD?

WHO WAS LOUIS PASTEUR?

Louis Pasteur (1822–1895) was a French scientist who showed that invisible organisms can spoil food and cause disease. Pasteurization, the process he invented of making liquids hot enough to kill any harmful organisms without destroying their food value, is still used today, particularly in milk production. It is used to kill bacteria that can cause tuberculosis in humans.

It was while studying the fermentation process of wine and vinegar that he made his greatest discovery: by heating wine to about 60°C (140°F) he killed off the unwanted yeast cells that caused the product to spoil.

• FACT FILE •

Pasteur developed a vaccine for the killer disease rabies, which he developed from the brain tissue of infected animals. Pasteur was hailed as a hero when he cured a boy who had been bitten by a rabid dog.

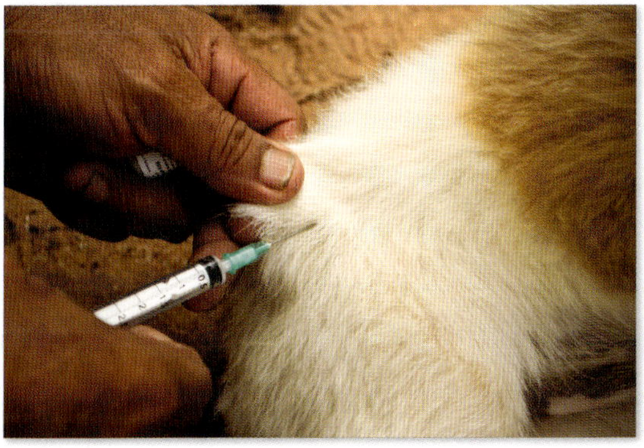

In one famous experiment, Louis Pasteur proved that germs could only come from other germs.

WHO DISCOVERED X-RAYS?

In November 1895, German physicist Wilhelm Roentgen found that by passing electricity through a vacuum he produced a new type of high energy radiation. He called the radiation 'X' (for unknown) rays. Roentgen also discovered that a beam of X-rays could pass through the body to produce an image on a photographic plate. Roentgen found that while bones appeared as clear images on the plate, soft tissues, such as muscle and skin, were much less distinct. Within weeks, Roentgen's discovery was greeted as one of the most significant in the history of medicine. For the first time doctors could look inside the living body without having to cut it open.

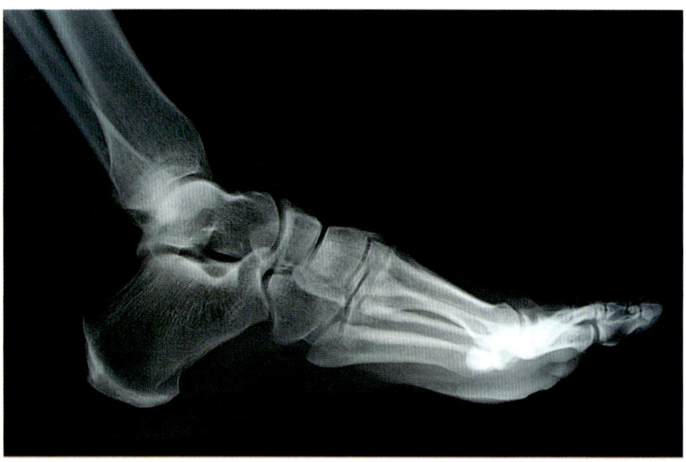

Today X-rays are used routinely to detect broken bones and other disorders.

• FACT FILE •

X-rays are also used in combination with computers in Computed Tomography (CT) Scanners. CT scanners produce images in the form of body 'slices' that show both hard and soft tissues.

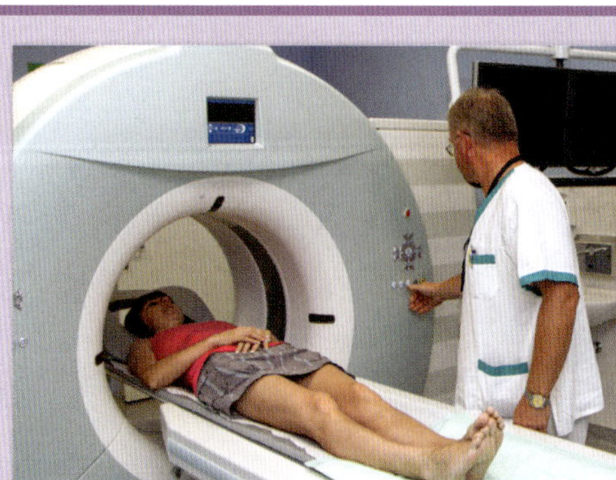

WHO WAS MARIE CURIE?

Marie Curie (1867–1934) was a Polish physicist. Born Marie Sklodowska, she worked as a child-minder to support herself while she studied at university in Paris. It was here that she met and married the French scientist Pierre Curie in 1895. In 1898, the Curies discovered the radioactive elements radium, thorium and polonium, named after Marie's homeland. In 1903, they shared the Nobel Prize for Physics with Henri Becquerel. In 1911, Marie Curie was awarded the Nobel Prize for Chemistry for her continuing work on radium and radioactivity. Doctors found that radium could be used to treat cancer through radiotherapy.

MARIE CURIE HAD NO IDEA HOW DANGEROUS HER DISCOVERY WAS AND USED TO CARRY RADIUM IN HER POCKET WHILE WORKING IN THE LABORATORY.

• FACT FILE •

Radiology is a branch of medicine that allows doctors to see inside the human body. They do so by using X-rays, MRI scans, PET scans and ultrasound, among other techniques. This allows specialists to diagnose and treat a range of diseases.

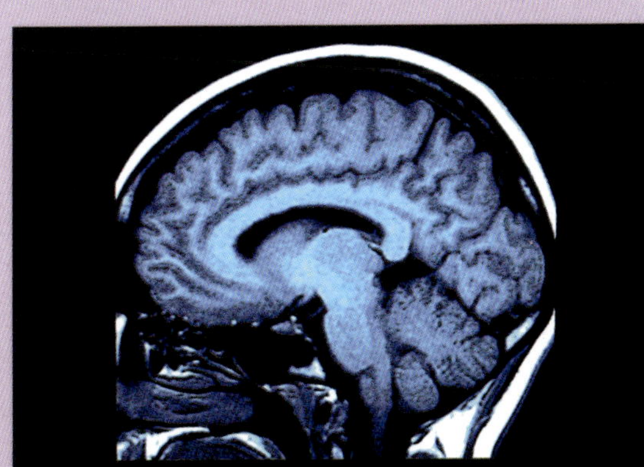

WHO DISCOVERED THAT $E=MC^2$?

The equation $E=mc^2$ was the work of Albert Einstein (1879–1955), a German-Swiss-American mathematician. Einstein was born in Germany and attended college in Zurich, Switzerland. In 1901, he got a job at the Swiss Patent Office, and became a Swiss citizen. In his spare time he worked on difficult mathematical problems. When his work became well known, he returned to Germany. In 1933, he went to the United States and, in 1940, he became a US citizen. Somewhere among Einstein's maths is the simple formula $E=mc^2$. This means that matter (m) can be converted into energy (E), and that the amount of energy will be equal to the amount of matter times the speed of light (c) squared. The speed of light is about 300,000 km (185,000 miles) per second, so that mc^2 makes for a lot of energy. Einstein's formula summarizes what happens when an atom bomb explodes.

DID YOU KNOW THAT EINSTEIN'S BRAIN WAS STOLEN DURING HIS AUTOPSY?

FACT FILE

The speed of light was central to Einstein's thinking. One morning, travelling to work by bus, Einstein glanced at the Town Hall clock – if the bus suddenly accelerated to the speed of light, then the clock would appear to stop. The relative motion between observer and observed is at the heart of Einstein's two theories of relativity.

WHO DISCOVERED GENES?

In the 1800s a monk named Gregor Mendel experimented with characteristics in pea plants by cross-fertilizing plants with different traits. He kept a careful track of the traits displayed by the pea plants, discovering that the characteristics from the parent plants were inherited by the progeny plants in specific patterns. Mendel also discovered during his experiments that certain genes seemed more dominant than others. For example if a pea with a white flower is cross-fertilized with a pea with a pink flower, the resulting flowers will all be pink. This is obvious in human beings. For example, if a child has a gene for brown eyes from one parent and a gene for blue eyes from the other, the child will always have brown eyes. This is because the gene for brown eyes is a dominant gene.

Curly hair, freckles, dimples and unattached earlobes – all of these are carried by dominant genes.

FACT FILE

Chromosomes are tiny threads that are present in all cells apart from red blood cells. They contain all the information for an entire person to develop. There are 46 chromosomes in each cell. They come in 22 pairs, plus another special pair that determines the person's sex.

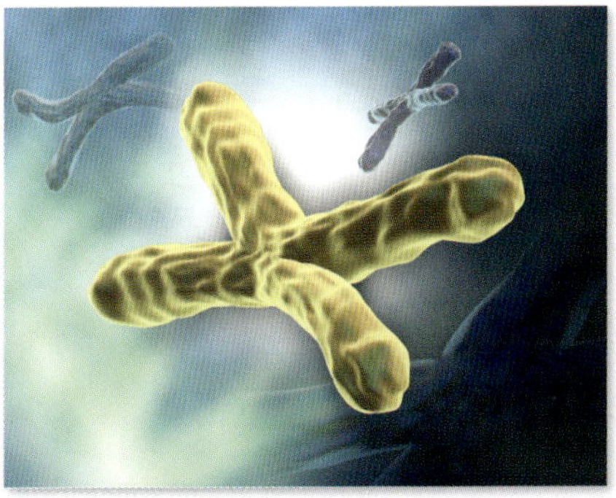

WHO DISCOVERED THE STRUCTURE OF DNA?

Molecular biologist, Francis Crick and biochemist, James Watson, are credited with the discovery of the structure of DNA. Crick studied at Cambridge University and during World War II designed anti-shipping mines. Watson studied viruses at the University of Indiana, where he received his doctorate in 1950.

By 1950, scientists knew what DNA was made from, but they had no idea of its shape. Crick and Watson made many models of what they thought it might look like. Finally they came up with a double helix, shaped like a long, twisted ladder. In 1962, the pair of them shared the Nobel Prize for Medicine.

The first DNA and molecule plate model

?

DID YOU KNOW THAT SCIENTISTS USED TO CALL MICROSCOPES 'FLEA GLASSES'? THAT'S BECAUSE THEY WERE USED TO OBSERVE SMALL INSECTS.

FACT FILE

DNA strands look like a twisted ladder. Sections of DNA are called genes. All the instructions for growing a new human being are coded into the DNA molecule.

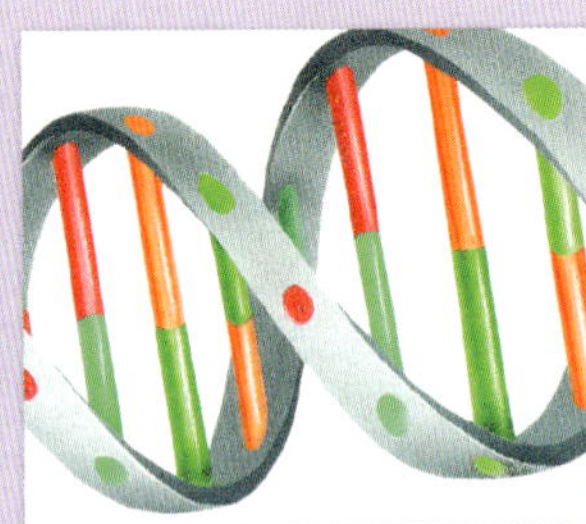

WHY ARE MICROSCOPES USED?

The word microscope is a combination of two Greek words, *mikros* or 'small' and *skopos* or 'watcher'. So this means that a microscope is a 'watcher of small' objects. It is an instrument that is used to see tiny things which are invisible to the naked eye.

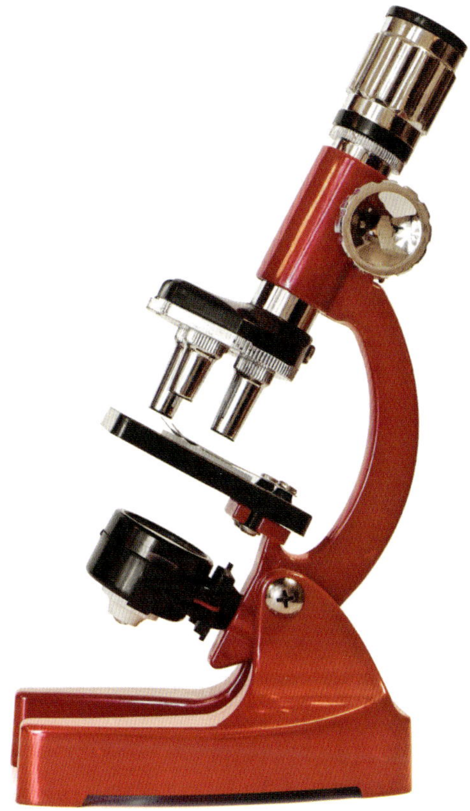

Normally an object appears larger the closer it is brought to the human eye. But when it is nearer than 25.5 cm (10 inches) it becomes blurred. It is said to be out of focus. Now if a simple convex lens is placed between the eye and the object, the object can be brought nearer than 25.5 cm (10 inches) and still remain in focus. Today the microscope is important to man in almost every form of industry, from dentistry to jewellery-making.

It was a Dutchman called Antonie van Leeuwenhoek (1632–1723) who discovered ground glass lenses, which he used to examine the world about him. In the 1670s he made his first crude microscope with a tiny lens. This allowed him to be the first person to see microscopic life such as bacteria.

• FACT FILE •

Some microscopes are so powerful they can magnify the smallest objects many thousands of times. These plant cells would be invisible to the human eye without the use of magnification.

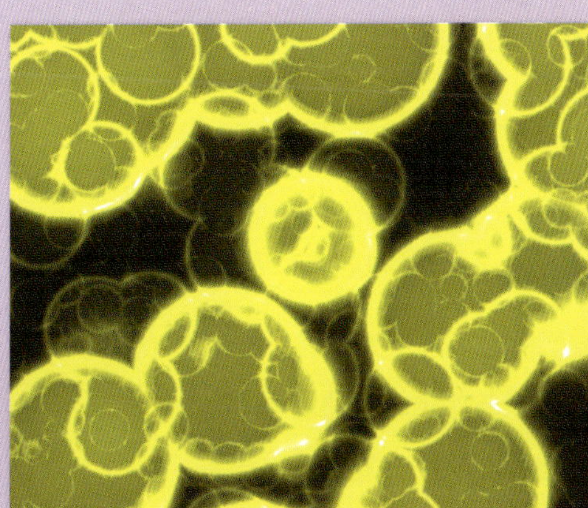

WHY IS LITMUS PAPER USED IN CHEMISTRY?

Litmus paper is a quick way to test a liquid to see whether it is acid or alkaline.

Dyes called indicators show very quickly if a substance dissolved in water is acid or alkaline. One of these dyes is litmus. If a piece of paper impregnated with litmus is dipped into a solution, it immediately turns red if the solution is acid. If the solution is alkaline, the litmus turns blue.

A similar dye to litmus is present in some red vegetables, such as red cabbage and beetroot and this dye changes colour in the same way during cooking. If your tap water is hard, or alkaline, the vegetables will be coloured a deep purplish-blue.

Acids and alkalines are measured using the pH scale, which runs from 0 to 14. Acids have a pH less than 7, 7 is neutral, and alkalines have a pH higher than 7.

• FACT FILE •

Bee stings are acidic. An acid is neutralized by an alkali, so as to reduce the painful effects of a bee sting. Soap is alkaline and will therefore help to lessen the effect of the sting if it is rubbed on the skin.

HOW ARE CRYSTALS FORMED?

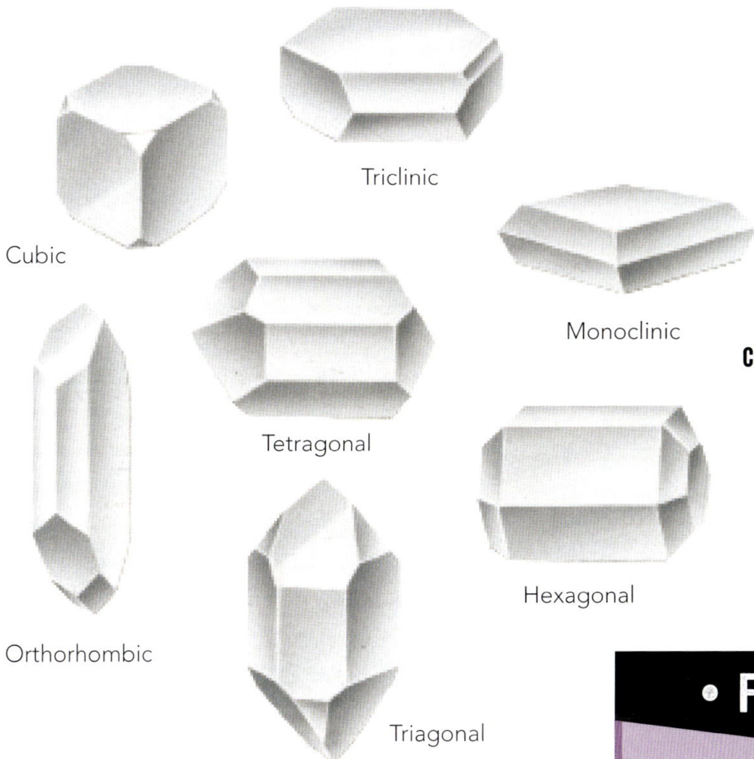

DIFFERENT CRYSTAL SHAPES

Crystals are formed from dissolved substances, or when molten substances cool slowly. As the solutions evaporate or the melted materials cool, their atoms are forced closer together, producing a crystal. The crystal gradually grows as the process continues. Some crystals grow into complicated and beautiful shapes, which are often very brightly coloured.

Crystals are solid substances that have their atoms arranged in regular patterns. Most naturally occurring substances form crystals under the right conditions, although they are not always apparent.

• FACT FILE •

Snowflakes are made up of millions of ice crystals. If you were to look at them under a microscope each would appear to be a different pattern.

MATERIALS AND THEIR USES

CONTENTS

WHEN WAS CLAY FIRST USED?

Clay is believed to have been used to make ceramic objects for at least 15,000 years. As early as 5,000 years ago people learned how to make their clay pots stronger and watertight, using fire. People soon discovered that by burning clay, its properties changed completely.

The uses of clay broadened from making small vessels to building materials. Clay-based bricks and tiles were among the first composite materials. Egyptian wall paintings of 5,000 years ago show clay workers making such bricks and pots.

The more adept people became at using clay, the more intricate the products they made. Some pottery dating back thousands of years shows a high artistic quality in its production; examples of this are common from the Far East. Through the ages, the use of clay in construction increased even more. Still today, ceramics is a huge industry world-wide.

FRAGMENTS OF CLAY POTS HAVE BEEN FOUND THAT DATE BACK TO THE NEOLITHIC PERIOD. THAT'S OVER 10,000 YEARS AGO!

• FACT FILE •

Ancient brick-makers fired bricks in kilns to produce building materials for structures that were intended to last.

HOW ARE CRAYONS MADE?

A STUDY IN AMERICA RANKED CRAYONS AT 18 OUT OF 20 OF THE MOST RECOGNIZABLE SMELLS TO ADULTS.

Crayons today are made from clay – a fine-grained, heavy soil – the same material that is used for making many pots. The clay is mixed with a pigment, to give it colour, and wax to prevent it drying out. Hundreds of colours are now available.

Before wax crayons were made, the most popular form were called chalks. White chalk was made from the stone of the same name (a form of limestone), black chalk from shale and red chalk from red ochre. The stone was ground, mixed with a liquid to bind it together and then dried into sticks. Pastels, which can come in many colours, are mixed with gum rather than wax or water.

• FACT FILE •

Limestone has built up under the sea over millions of years from the shells of tiny creatures called formanifera, which settled on the sea floor after they died and built up into a layer miles thick.

WHAT IS GLUE?

Traditionally, glue is made from boiling up the bones, skins and other parts of animals such as fish or horses in order to extract the gelatin, which is then purified and concentrated to make a sticky substance that will form a bond as it dries. There are now many different types of glue, made from plant material or minerals such as petrol, as well as different kinds of synthetic glue. One of the simplest glues is flour-and-water paste, while traditional wallpaper paste is made using starch. Latex adhesives were originally made from the latex extracted from rubber trees, but synthetic forms are now also available. Another type of synthetic glue is epoxy resin, in which the user mixes an adhesive substance with equal quantities of a hardener. The two substances react chemically together, causing the adhesive to set rapidly.

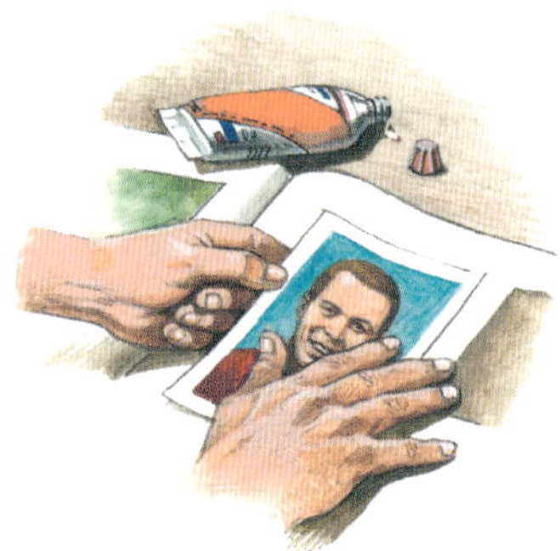

Glues are widely used in many industries, such as furniture-making and food-packaging.

FACT FILE

In order to protect it and make it last longer, paper money, such as dollar bills or £10 notes, is 'sized' with glue. If this were not done, the ink would rub off and the notes would quickly get very dirty.

WHERE WAS GLASS FIRST USED?

The first glass vessels were made in about 1500 BCE in Mesopotamia (modern Iraq) and Egypt. Bits of highly decorative glass vessels have been found in some tombs in the Valley of the Kings in Egypt, including a late 15th-century BCE bottle in the tomb of Pharaoh Amenhopis II. At this time glass vessels were formed around a core that was then removed, as the technique of blowing glass had not yet been invented. The Egyptians also used coloured glass inlays on the coffins and mummy cases of pharoahs and other important people, as can be seen on the gold mask of Tutankhamen.

The Romans learned how to make blow pipes, and subsequently blown glass, in about 30 BCE, which made glass vessels both easier and cheaper to manufacture.

Interestingly, although it appears solid, glass is, in fact, a liquid that has been cooled very quickly to prevent it forming crystals. It moves very slowly, but glass windows that are very old are thicker at the bottom because gravity has gradually pulled the glass down.

• FACT FILE •

It is very easy to recycle glass. It is simply broken up and melted, before being shaped again in the normal way.

THE OLDEST EXAMPLES OF GLASS ARE EGYPTIAN BEADS DATING FROM 12,000 BCE.

WHEN WAS PAPER FIRST MADE?

The first paper was made about 2,000 years ago in China, by a man called Ts'ai Lun. He took the stringy inner bark of the Mulberry tree and pounded it in water until it became a mass of flattened threads. He then placed this pulped solution onto a flat tray of fine bamboo strips.

The water was allowed to drain through the bamboo, and the threads in the bamboo were left to dry. The dried result was a flat, fibrous material considered to be the very first paper. As with all new discoveries, improvements were gradually made. One of these was to brush starch over the paper.

The technique of making paper was taken to Russia and the Middle East by Chinese traders and from there it spread to Europe. Paper making was revolutionary in the spread of knowledge and mass production began. The first continuous paper-making machine was developed in France by Louis Robert in 1798. At the start of the 19th century, the Fourdrinier brothers developed the idea further in London.

Nowadays we produce wood-free paper in an attempt to limit the damage to our environment.

• FACT FILE •

The Chinese had another secret – they were the only people who knew how to make silk. European traders would make the long journey to take silk back to Europe.

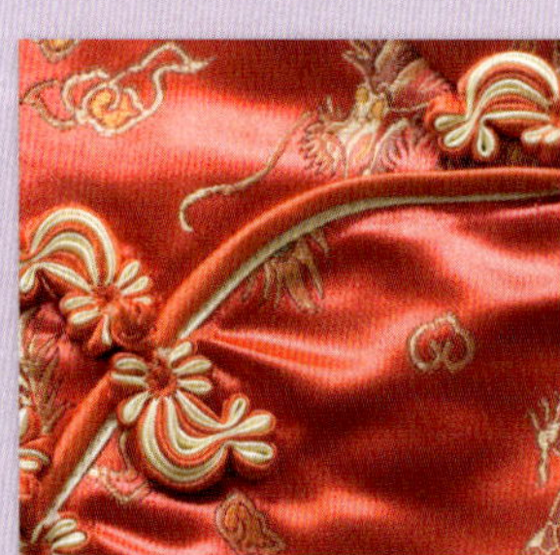

?

DID YOU KNOW THAT THE FIRST BOOK TO BE PRINTED MECHANICALLY IS SAID TO BE THE GUTENBERG BIBLE? IT WAS PRINTED IN GERMANY IN AROUND 1455.

WHEN WERE THE FIRST BOOKS MADE?

Medieval choir book

The first books were made about 4,000 years ago by the Egyptians who took flattened layers of papyrus stems to make sheets. The 'books' they made were collections of rolled papyrus sheets – very different from a book of today. In the middle of the fifth century, parchment (sheep skin) replaced papyrus. Parchment sheets were placed on top of one another and bound down one side with leather thongs.

But it was in the Middle Ages that books as we know them today evolved. Vellum (calf skin) was made into sheets, and each piece was folded down the middle. Four vellum sheets made eight leaves and was considered a section. Unlike parchment, vellum was thick enough to be written on both sides. Finished sections were sewn together down the back fold (the spine) and covered with wooden boards front and back. The boards and spine were then covered with leather; the result was a book similar to that of today.

• FACT FILE •

In about 500 CE monks would spend endless hours on illuminated handwritten books. The work was slow and painstaking, but worthwhile because it was another way to show dedication to God.

WHEN WERE STAINED GLASS WINDOWS INTRODUCED?

Historical documents and excavations have discovered that stained glass was around as far back as the 12th century. These are true stained glass windows that tell a pictorial story and are considered the invention of Western Europe.

Religious writings dating as far back as 240 CE mention the existence of tinted glass in windows of the early Christian basilicas.

Stained glass windows of medieval times were basic in their manufacture. The window opening was filled with thin sheets of marble or wood, with holes pierced through. Tinted glass was placed in the holes; this was known as a mosaic window. Leading was also used to join pieces of glass together to make attractive patterns in the windows.

• FACT FILE •

Circular turrets on medieval castles had very unusual windows – they were very narrow slits. Because they were built as fortresses the windows were designed to minimize the chance of being hit by arrows.

HOW ARE MIRRORS MADE?

The Hall of Mirrors at the Palace of Versailles, in France, has one wall on which 357 mirrors stretch from floor to ceiling.

Mirrors are pieces of glass that have been coated with a reflective material on the back, so that when a beam of light strikes the surface none of it is absorbed. The beam of light is actually reflected away again.

The beam of light is reflected at exactly the same angle as it struck the mirror, but in the opposite direction. This can be visualized if you imagine a snooker ball striking the cushion of the table and bouncing back at an angle. Mirrors are used in many ways – for example in telescopes, flashlights, headlights of cars and lamps in lighthouses.

• FACT FILE •

Mirrors are used in lighthouses to help reflect the light a long way to help ships out at sea. Some lighthouses have their own generators so that the light does not go out.

WHEN DID GOLD MINING BEGIN?

Although the time cannot be pinpointed exactly, it is widely believed that gold mining extends back about 5,000 years. The first gold was mined in Egypt, which remained the centre of gold production until the first or second century CE. Egyptian wall paintings show gold mining in its various stages. In those days, gold was panned from water; this was achieved by sifting out the lighter sands in the water to leave the heavier, gold particles behind. By 3,000 BCE gold rings were used as a form of payment. With the exception of coins, gold was used only for decorative purposes.

Around 2,000 BCE mine shafts were constructed to obtain gold ore found in pockets deep in the ground; the Greeks and Romans were adept at this.

• FACT FILE •

Gold standard was a monetary system in which the standard unit of currency was a fixed quantity of gold. It was first put into operation in Great Britain in 1821.

?

DID YOU KNOW THAT PURE GOLD IS SO SOFT THAT YOU CAN MOULD IT IN YOUR HANDS?

HOW IS COAL FORMED?

The hardest and purest form of coal is called anthracite.

Coal is formed by the compressed remains of plants that lived in bogs 250–350 million years ago. This was during the Carboniferous Period, when primitive animals first appeared on the land. Coal formed from the remains of tree ferns and other primitive trees, which were covered with mud and sand and buried as new rock was laid down. Very gradually, over millions of years, this material turned into coal.

A similar process is taking place today in peat bogs, where the rotting remains of heather form peat. When the peat is dried it burns in a similar way to coal. In some parts of the world a soft shale, called brown coal, is mined.

• FACT FILE •

Before we had central heating to warm our houses most people had coal fires, and matches were a quick and easy way to light them.

WHERE WOULD YOU FIND CARBON?

Carbon is found in all living things: it is one of the most familiar and important chemical elements yet it makes up only 0.032 per cent of the Earth's crust. Carbon is the main component of such fuels as coal, petroleum and natural gas. Carbon is also found in most plastics, many of which are derived from carbon fuels. Carbon has the chemical symbol C. Pure carbon occurs in four forms: (1) diamond (2) graphite (as used in pencils) (3) amorphous carbons and (4) fullerenes. The four forms have different crystalline structures – that is, their atoms are arranged differently. The various forms of carbon differ greatly in hardness and other properties, depending on how their atoms are arranged.

• FACT FILE •

Diamond is the hardest naturally occurring substance and one of the most valuable. Natural diamonds form in the rock beneath the Earth's crust where high temperature and pressure cause carbon atoms to make strong bonds with four other carbon atoms each, and to crystallize.

?

DID YOU KNOW THAT THE 'LEAD' IN YOUR PENCIL ISN'T LEAD AT ALL? WHEN GRAPHITE WAS FIRST DISCOVERED, SCIENTISTS MISTOOK IT FOR LEAD INSTEAD OF CARBON, AND WE HAVE BEEN CALLING IT LEAD EVER SINCE – IN PENCILS, AT LEAST.

WHERE WOULD SOOT BE HARMFUL?

Soot can be harmful to the respiratory system, particularly the lungs. Soot is a black or dark brown substance found in smoke, and mainly consists of carbon particles. These particles have a diameter less than the width of a human hair. They form when carbon-containing fuels, such as coal, wood or oil do not burn completely.

Airborne soot is a form of air pollution. It sticks to any surface it touches. It can also cause widespread damage to property. Smoke blowing through a city leaves soot on buildings, making them look dingy. This soot can eventually damage the surfaces of the buildings by chemically reacting with them.

The smaller soot particles are, the more harmful they become, because they can travel deeper into the lungs.

• FACT FILE •

Although soot can be a pollutant, it is also valuable as a pigment. Two kinds of soot used as pigments are bister and lampblack.

WHEN WAS THE FIRST PLASTIC MADE?

Plastics are made by a chemical process called polymerization. Nineteenth-century chemists understood the making of plastics. The first plastic, vinyl chloride, was made in 1838, closely followed by styrene in 1839, acrylics in 1843 and polyester in 1847. However, the vast potential for their use was not understood. Later that century, cheaper, substitute manufacturing materials were needed. In 1869, John Hyatt discovered celluloid when looking for a substitute for ivory. This revolutionary material was tough and malleable; it started a wave of chemists developing new synthetic materials. In 1909, Leo Bakeland was responsible for the biggest development when he discovered phenolformaldehyde. This material was cheap to produce and could be moulded into any shape. He called it Bakelite and it was the first synthetic material to be mass-produced. The space technology of the late 1960s, among other developments, has been applied by scientists to develop new plastics and other synthetic materials.

A toy duck is a good example of how easily plastic can be moulded.

Now that we are in the 21st century, we need to conserve our environment, so new biodegradable materials, are constantly being sought.

• FACT FILE •

Plastic is an ideal material for producing rainwear. It is water-resistant, air-permeable, shrink-resistant and can be easily wiped down.

WHERE WOULD YOU USE THERMOPLASTICS?

Polytetrafluoroethylene is a thermoplastic that resists heat and chemicals and slides easily. It is used for cable insulation, bearings, valve seats, gaskets and frying-pan coatings.

Although there are hundreds of different plastics, all of them belong to one of two basic types, based on how they behave when heated. These types are: thermosetting plastics and thermoplastics. Thermoplastics can be melted and re-formed again and again. Their polymer chains do not form cross-links. So, the chains can move freely each time the plastic material is heated.

Thermoplastics are widely used because they are easier to handle. They also require less time to set – as little as ten seconds. Thermoplastics can be dispersed in liquids to produce durable paints and lacquers. Because their molecules can slide slowly past one another, some thermoplastics tend to lose their shape when exposed to constant pressure over a long period of time.

• FACT FILE •

Products made from thermosetting plastics include pot handles, trays for sterilizing medical instruments and parts for aeroplanes and spacecraft.

WHAT IS LEATHER?

Leather is made of cured animal skin with the hair removed. Humankind's first use of animal skins was to wrap up in uncured skins to keep off the cold and wet. Hanging the skins in the smoke near a fire prevented them from rotting. Later, soaking skins in water with the bark, leaves or galls of certain trees had the same effect and also softened the hides, making it easier to shape them and remove the hair, as well as change their colour. The substance that preserves the hides is tannin, and the process is called tanning. Modern synthetic chemicals are also now used, as well as chemical dyes that can give the leather bright colours.

• FACT FILE •

Among the animals whose skin is used for leather are calves, pigs, horses, sheep, goats, deer, ostriches, alligators, crocodiles, lizards, snakes, seals, whales, sharks and walruses.

WHAT WAS THE FIRST TYPE OF SHOE?

The first shoes were probably an early prototype for sandals, with soles made of hide, bark, wood or woven grass, which were bound to the feet and ankles with strips of hide. The earliest shoe uncovered by archaeologists, a slipper, was found in Oregon, in the northwestern United States and is thought to be 10,000 years old

In 1991, archaeologists discovered Ötzi the Iceman, in the Alps. The remains preserved in the ice are thought to be about 5,000 years old. He was wearing shoes with bearskin soles, deerskin insteps and uppers made of tanned chamois or cowhide and bark. They were stuffed with grass for warmth. The ancient Minoans also wore footwear: a fresco at Knossos on Crete (c. 1500 BCE) shows two athletes wearing what look like shoes and shin guards.

Several pairs of sandals with leather or papyrus soles with two leather straps were found in the tomb of the ancient Egyptian Tutankhamen. It is reasonable to suppose that less prosperous Egyptians also wore sandals for protection.

• FACT FILE •

An animal has no need for any shoes. Its feet have been specially designed with a thick, tough leathery sole for protection.

WHY DO WE NEED OIL?

Fossil fuels, which include oil, coal and natural gas, were formed millions of years ago when prehistoric plants and animals died. Their decaying bodies were pressed under layers of rock and earth and became fossilized. Life as we know it today would not be possible without fossil fuels. Not only are they burned to supply heat and energy to our homes, but by forming the fuel for power stations, they also supply most of our electricity. Also, fossil fuels can be processed to produce many other useful materials, including plastics, dyes and bitumen.

Geologists know what kinds of rocks are likely to contain or cover oil deposits. When they find a likely area on land or at sea, test drilling is carried out to find out if there is any oil beneath the surface.

The carbon and hydrogen in oil can be used to make petrol. This is the most common fuel used to power our cars.

FACT FILE

Helicopters are an oil rig's lifeline. They not only bring workers food and supplies, but they can also airlift a person to hospital should they have an accident or be taken ill.

HOW CAN WAX BE BOTH NATURAL AND SYNTHETIC?

Wax can be obtained from many fruits, vegetables and plants. Waxes are also produced by animals and are found in minerals and petroleum. There are also synthetic, or man-made waxes. We acquire wax from many different sources.

Carnauba wax is obtained from the leaves of the carnauba palm tree of Brazil. It is a brown wax used in records, floor dressings and candles. Bayberry wax, from the berries of the shrub, is also used for making candles. Worker bees secrete wax that they use in making their honeycombs. This is used in cosmetics, church candles, polishes, crayons and artificial flowers. Wool wax from wool-bearing animals is called lanolin and it used in some ointments, cosmetics and soaps.

FACT FILE

Inside a hive, the bees store their honey in a network of wax that is called a honeycomb. Each one is made up of thousands of little six-sided cells. The bees feed on the honey during the cold winter months.

?

DID YOU KNOW THAT MORE THAN 90 PER CENT OF ALL COMMERCIAL WAX USED TODAY IS PETROLEUM WAX. IT HAS A WIDE VARIETY OF USES BECAUSE IT IS ODOURLESS, TASTELESS AND CHEMICALLY INACTIVE.

WHY IS STEEL AN IMPORTANT MATERIAL?

Iron has a lot of carbon in it, which makes it crack very easily. If some carbon is removed, iron turns into super-strong steel. An enormous range of items can be made from steel, from tiny paperclips to huge girders forming the frames for skyscrapers. One very useful property of steel is that it can be recycled and used over and over again. Steel is the most important ingredient for making cars. Most screws, nails, nuts and bolts are made of steel and the huge cranes that make modern construction possible are built of steel. Also steel girders form the skeleton of new buildings.

THE EIFFEL TOWER IS 15CM (6IN) TALLER IN SUMMER THAN IT IS IN WINTER! THIS IS BECAUSE STEEL AND IRON EXPAND WHEN HEATED.

• FACT FILE •

Stainless steel contains small amounts of nickel and chromium to make a metal that does not corrode. Many everyday things are made of stainless steel such as: cutlery, taps, sewing pins and needles, and scissors.

WHERE WOULD YOU SEE RUST?

Rust is a brownish-red substance that forms on the surface of iron or steel when it is exposed to damp air. The term used alone means iron rust, which consists mainly of hydrated iron oxide. Rust not only corrodes the surface but also weakens the metal. Long exposure to air and moisture will cause nails to rust off, and rust holes to form in sheet iron. Iron can be mixed with other chemical elements to create rust-resistant metal called stainless steel. Iron and steel that are not rust resistant should be kept dry or coated with a substance, such as chrome or paint that will resist the action of oxygen. Polished tools may be easily protected if wiped with a cloth soaked in oil. Coating metal objects with heavy greases or spray-on plastics, or wrapping them in special chemically treated paper, also prevents rust.

Rust is formed by the union of oxygen in the air with iron by a process called oxidation.

• FACT FILE •

You would not want to eat with rusty cutlery, so chromium is added to steel to make an alloy called stainless steel. Unlike other metals, stainless steel will not react with acids in foods.

COMMUNICATION AND TRAVEL

CONTENTS

WHEN WAS MORSE CODE DEVELOPED?

Morse code is a messaging system that uses two kinds of signal, a short one called a dot, and a long one called a dash. The signals are sent via telegraphs. A transmitter sends a coded message in long and short bursts of radio waves along a wire; the receiver then translates the dots and dashes into their representative letters, numbers and words. Samuel Morse (1791–1872) was an American engineer who developed this system. He conceived the idea of some sort of communication via telegraph in 1832. After several years of work on the idea, Morse perfected it in 1838.

However, at that time, telegraph lines did not exist across land, so there was no way Morse could put his code to use on a practical scale. It was 1843 before the US government allocated a sum of money to construct a telegraph line between Washington and Baltimore. Morse sent the first message along the lines in 1844.

?

DID YOU KNOW THAT MORSE CODE IS STILL USED TO THIS DAY? IT IS SOMETIMES USED FOR COMMUNICATION BETWEEN COAST GUARDS AND VESSELS AT SEA, AND IN AVIATION.

• FACT FILE •

S •••
O – – –
S •••

Morse code was used a lot during the war because it was a quick and easy way of sending messages. Probably the most famous signal was SOS, a distress signal that actually stands for 'Save Our Souls'.

WHEN WAS BRAILLE INVENTED?

The Braille system was invented in 1829 by a blind man called Louis Braille. He developed a system that would allow blind people to read and write. It is today one of the most widely used alphabets for the blind.

In the Braille system, each letter of the alphabet is represented by a combination of dots. These combinations are punched onto paper, so that they appear as raised bumps. A blind person reads the dots by moving their fingers over the bumps, recognizing each letter to spell out the words.

There were earlier systems of reading for the blind. Even as far back as 1517 alphabetic letters were engraved onto blocks of wood for the blind to read. This system was good to read by, but the drawback was that the blind could not see how to form the letters when they wanted to write.

LOUIS BRAILLE ESTABLISHED HIS SYSTEMS WHEN HE WAS STILL IN HIS TEENS.

• FACT FILE •

Semaphore is another means of communicating, by using flags. Different flag positions represent different letters and numbers. It was widely used between ships sailing near each other in the days before radio.

WHY ARE MEANS OF COMMUNICATION ALWAYS DEVELOPING?

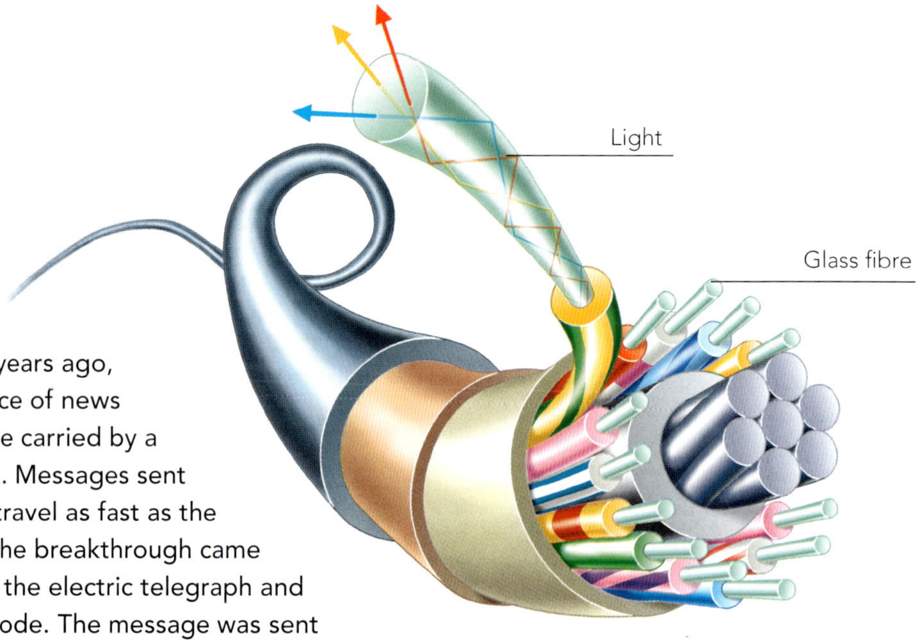

Only a few hundred years ago, the fastest way a piece of news could travel was to be carried by a person on horseback. Messages sent overseas could only travel as fast as the fastest sailing ship. The breakthrough came with the invention of the electric telegraph and messages in Morse code. The message was sent down a wire in bursts of electric current.

Today, however, images of written documents, sound recordings or television pictures can be flashed around the globe in less than a second by means of satellites and radio communications. Several satellites, in different orbits, are required to give coverage over the whole globe, and different satellites are used to reflect signals for different media, such as telephone messages and television pictures.

• FACT FILE •

A great amount of communication these days is carried out via satellites. Radio, telephone and television messages are transmitted around the world with incredible speed. Such satellites orbit the Earth so that they appear to be in the same place all the time – even though the Earth is spinning round.

WHERE WOULD YOU USE A CARBON TRANSMITTER?

A carbon transmitter is found in the handset of a landline telephone. It consists of a microphone, which produces an electric copy of the user's voice, and a receiver, which duplicates the voice of the person on the other end of the line. Mobile phones are two-way radios that convert the sound to radio waves, which travel through the air until they reach a receiver at a nearby base station. The base station sends your call through the network until it reaches the person you are calling. When you get a call, a nearby base station sends out radio waves that are detected by your mobile, where the signals are converted into voice or data.

ONE STORY GOES THAT TELEPHONE WIRES USED TO BE RANKED BY THEIR TASTINESS TO RATS AND MICE.

• FACT FILE •

Alexander Graham Bell (1847–1922), a Scottish-born inventor and educator, is best known for his invention of the telephone. Bell was 27 years old when he worked out the principle of transmitting speech electrically, and was 29 when his basic telephone patent was granted in 1876.

WHAT WAS THE FIRST MEANS OF TRANSPORT?

Early humans had to rely on their own muscle-power to carry objects, but over thousands of years tamed animals, such as horses, oxen and donkeys, elephants and camels. In order to be able to transport more goods than an animal could carry on its back, sledges and hurdles that could be pulled behind the animal were eventually invented, as well as such instruments as ploughs to make agriculture easier. Where sledges were not suitable, such as on rough ground or sand, heavy objects were rolled along on top of logs, continually taken from behind the object as it passed and placed in front of it. It is thought that stones for both the pyramids and Stonehenge may have been moved using this technique. Eventually, someone realized that attaching the logs, or sections of log, to the object would be more efficient and the wheel was born.

The oldest known wheel was found in what used to be Mesopotamia (modern-day Iraq, Syria and Kuwait) and dates to around 3500 BCE.

FACT FILE

Over the thousands of years since it was first invented, the wheel has developed to become more durable, stronger, lighter and much more comfortable for passengers and drivers.

WHO INVENTED THE BICYCLE?

The first designs for people-propelled two-wheeled vehicles date from about 1790. German Karl von Drais made an improved model, the draisienne, in about 1817. It had a handlebar to steer the front wheel, but no pedals.

Kirkpatrick Macmillan, a Scottish blacksmith, added pedals to the front wheel in 1839, creating the bicycle, although it had no chain and no gears.

In the 1870s, new designs were made, including the penny-farthing. In 1872, Englishman J. Starley added a chain drive linking the front and rear wheels and in 1885 he produced the first commercial safety bicycle. The invention of pneumatic tyres in 1888 made the machines more comfortable to ride. Modern cycles are made of light alloy and cycling is very popular for health and environmental reasons.

Penny-farthing

Modern bicycle

• FACT FILE •

Over the years, bicycles have been adapted in many different ways. These wheelchairs are specially built for various sports, including track and field events.

WHEN WAS THE HEYDAY OF CANAL BUILDING?

People have used canals to transport heavy goods for thousands of years. It is believed that the first canals were built to join together existing rivers to make a transport route. Indeed, the city of Venice in Italy was built on a system of canals rather than roads; 6,000 years ago an impressive system of canals was constructed in the Aztec city of Tenochtitlan.

However, the heyday of canal building was much more recent. The Industrial Revolution was responsible for the upsurge in canal building. There was a huge need during this era for cheap and easy ways to transport goods from factories to ports. Horse-drawn and steam-powered canal boats were faster than carrying cargo by horse-drawn carts along the road.

Panama Canal

The longest canal in the world is the Grand Canal in China. It stretches 1,776km (1104 miles) and has 24 locks.

FACT FILE

Locks are an essential feature of any canal that needs to gain or lose height. A lock has gates that can be closed to control the water level in a section of the canal. Water is let into or taken from the section, raising or lowering the vessel inside.

WHEN WAS THE FIRST METAL BRIDGE BUILT?

It was the Industrial Revolution that brought about the introduction of metal bridges. In the past, bridges were constructed of stone and timber, which were available in large quantities. Iron was used because it was much stronger than either wood or stone, and was, on the whole, less expensive to produce. Bridges made from timber or masonry became fewer and fewer.

The first-ever metal bridge was built in England in 1779. The Coalbrookdale Bridge, which spanned the River Severn, was designed by Thomas Pritchard and built by Andrew Darby. This bridge, the first to be built solely of iron, spanned almost 30m (100ft) across the river in an almost perfect semi-circular arrangement of cast-iron pieces.

• FACT FILE •

The drawbridge originated in medieval Europe as a defensive feature of castles and towns. It was operated by a counterweight and winch. In the late 19th century drawbridges began to be built specifically to aid navigation, Tower Bridge, in London, being a fine example.

HOW DOES A BOAT FLOAT?

The reason a boat, whatever size, can float on the surface of water is because it is the fluid itself that holds it up. The water offsets the force of gravity, which tries to pull everything to the centre of the Earth.

The upward push on a floating object is called 'buoyant force' or simply 'buoyancy'. If you want to feel this force just take a blown-up beach ball into the sea. You will feel that the water seems to push up on the ball.

When a solid body is placed in a liquid it pushes some of the fluid aside. If the solid is less dense than the fluid, it will float. A boat contains large quantities of air and is less dense than water. It weighs less than the water it pushes aside, so it floats.

• FACT FILE •

Helicopters are lifted into the air by their large rotating propellers or rotors. These work like narrow wings generating lift as they spin.

HOW DO AEROPLANES FLY?

Air pushing over the upper surface of an aircraft's wing reduces in pressure, allowing higher-pressure air underneath the wing to exert an upward force, thus enabling the aeroplane to fly.

Jet engines propel a plane just like a rocket, with a stream of hot gases.

As an aeroplane moves through the air, the air passes over the surface of its wings. These wings are shaped with a curved top surface and a flatter lower surface, which means that air passing over the top of the wing has to travel a little faster than that below the wing. This causes the pressure to lower above the wing, while the air pressure below pushes up. The end result is the lift that keeps the aeroplane in the air.

The tail surfaces of an aeroplane keep the wing at the proper angle to provide the right amount of lift. The power to propel the aeroplane along can come from the engine or, in the case of gliders, from rising air currents.

• FACT FILE •

Leonardo da Vinci (1452–1519) drew his plans for a helicopter hundreds of years before flying machines were even invented.

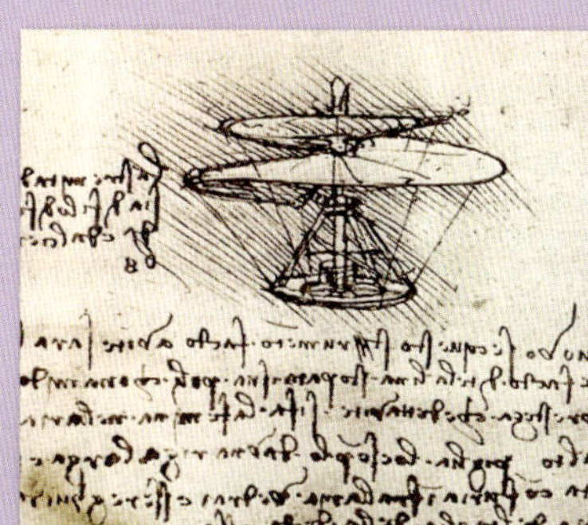

WHEN WAS THE FIRST AEROPLANE FLIGHT?

Gliders are pulled up to the correct altitude by powered aircraft and are then cut free.

The first ever powered, sustained and controlled aeroplane flight took place at the beginning of this century, on 17 December, 1903.

Orville Wright and his brother Wilbur both designed and built the plane for this historic flight. Orville piloted the first flight in the aircraft, aptly named the Flyer. He travelled 36.5m (120ft) through the air in 12 seconds; Wilbur managed 53m (175ft) in 12 seconds straight after this. They each had one more attempt: Orville flew (60m) 200ft in 15 seconds, before Wilbur recorded the longest flight of the day, travelling 260m (852ft) in 59 seconds.

A REGULAR FLIGHT ACROSS THE ATLANTIC TAKES EIGHT HOURS. CONCORDE COULD DO IT IN LESS THAN THREE!

FACT FILE

Concorde was a supersonic airliner. The sonic 'boom' it produced, together with noise and air pollution concerns, has limited the development of such aircraft.

WHICH PLANE HAS NO ENGINE?

A plane with no engine is called a glider. During the late 18th century, people made the first flights in the air using balloons, which were an early form of airship. After the first balloon flights, inventors tried to develop a heavier-than-air flying machine. Some inventors experimented with gliders. They studied birds' wings and discovered that the wings were curved. By building gliders with curved wings instead of flat ones, they could make the vehicles fly hundreds of metres.

Long-distance flight in a heavier-than-air machine did not become possible until the invention of an engine light enough but powerful enough to keep a plane in flight. The first such engines were four-stroke gasoline engines, developed during the 1880s and initially used to power bicycles, boats and carriages.

• FACT FILE •

In 1903, the brothers Orville and Wilbur Wright – two American bicycle makers – made the first successful powered aeroplane flights in history near Kitty Hawk, North Carolina.

WHY DO CARS HAVE ENGINES?

The very first vehicle able to run on the open road was powered by steam. However, it was not until the development of the internal combustion engine in the second half of the nineteenth century that motor transport began to be successful.

The first petrol-driven car

Internal combustion engines are usually fuelled by petrol or diesel. This fuel is burnt (or combusted) within metal cylinders. The burning fuel causes a piston to move up and down inside each cylinder. It is this upward and downward movement that is translated into a turning movement by the crankshaft, causing the axles and wheels to turn and the car to move forward.

The engine also powers an alternator, which generates an electrical current. This current is stored in the battery and is used for the car's lights, windscreen wipers, radio and other features, such as electric windows.

• FACT FILE •

Most petrol engines are quite noisy and give off harmful fumes. Quieter and cleaner electric cars are now being designed. However, their batteries need continually recharging so they are only used for short distances.

?

DID YOU KNOW THAT ELECTRIC CARS ARE GAINING IN POPULARITY? THIS IS BECAUSE, UNLIKE PETROL-ENGINE CARS, ELECTRIC CARS DO NOT EMIT EXHAUST FUMES.

WHERE WOULD YOU USE A CATALYTIC CONVERTER?

A catalytic converter is a device that reduces the exhaust pollutants produced by a motor vehicle engine. The engine's combustion process gives off carbon monoxide and other harmful chemical compounds. A substance called a catalyst in the converter helps change these pollutants into safer substances. The catalyst in most converters is a blend of the metals platinum, palladium and rhodium.

The catalytic converter is installed in an automobile's exhaust system. As the exhaust gases pass through the converter, the catalyst causes carbon monoxide and other pollutants to change into oxygen, nitrogen, water and carbon dioxide.

• FACT FILE •

Cars with catalytic converters must use fuel that is free of both lead and phosphorus. These substances coat the catalyst's surface, making it ineffective over time.

WHICH IS THE WORLD'S LONGEST ROAD SYSTEM?

The Pan-American Highway passes through many diverse ecosystems, from dense jungle to arid desert.

The world's longest road system is the Pan-American Highway, which criss-crosses Central and South America from the north of Mexico to the south of Chile and links 17 capital cities. The total system covers 47,516km (29,525 miles). It links up with roads in the United States of America and on to Canada, although these are not officially counted as part of the system.

The main aim of the network is to make the transportation of goods easier, both between the countries linked by the network and to the coasts for export elsewhere in the world – for example, coffee and soya from Brazil, beef and corn from Argentina and wine from Chile.

FACT FILE

Traffic congestion on streets and highways increases travelling times and can also make driving more dangerous. Scientists and engineers are developing systems to deal with congestion.

HOW CAN VEHICLES BE POWERED BY ELECTRICITY?

Electrically powered vehicles have been in use for many years. Powering cars with electricity does present certain problems, however, as the batteries are heavy and a car's energy requirement is high. This means that the distance an electric car can travel before it is recharged may be too low for many uses.

Where vehicles can obtain electrical energy from a fixed wire or track, there is no problem about the electrical supply. Electrically powered trains, such as ones used in France, are the fastest in the world.

Specially designed electrically powered wheelchairs and vehicles enable disabled people to move about at the same speed as a pedestrian. These are powered by rechargeable batteries.

• FACT FILE •

High-performance cars like the one below would not run very well if powered by electricity. They would not be able to travel very far or fast because the battery would not be powerful enough.

WHEN WAS THE HOVERCRAFT INVENTED?

?

DID YOU KNOW THAT THERE IS A HOVERCRAFT MUSEUM? IT IS BASED IN LEE-ON-THE-SOLENT IN HAMPSHIRE, ENGLAND AND HOLDS THE LARGEST COLLECTION OF HOVERCRAFT DESIGNS IN THE WORLD.

The hovercraft was invented in 1955 by the British scientist Christopher Cockerell. He decided to solve a problem that had been baffling scientists for 80 years. In the 1870s, the British engineer John Thornycroft began to design a ship that moved along on a cushion of air to reduce friction between the ship's hull and the water. He was unable to work out how to contain the cushion of air under the boat, but Cockerell solved this by affixing a rubber skirt to the bottom of the boat. This idea worked perfectly.

• FACT FILE •

A boat is a pretty large object, yet it floats easily on the surface of water. This is because the fluid actually holds it up. It is virtually impossible to sink a boat, unless the vessel springs a leak and takes on water.

WHO BUILT THE FIRST WORKING ROCKET?

According to historians, the Chinese built the first working rockets. They were also the first to use them for military purposes. In 1232, some ingenious military leader used arrows powered by small gunpowder rockets to successfully defend the city of K'ai-Fung-Foo against the invading Mongols.

During this time one Chinese official hit on the idea of using rockets to propel a man through the air. It was in about 1500 that Wan Hu fastened two kites together with a chair in between. He then tied a series of military rockets to the kites and asked an assistant to light the rockets. Not wanting to miss out on the chance for fame, Wan Hu decided to be his own test pilot. According to reports, he sat in the chair and gave the order to light the rockets. There was a lot of noise and a great burst of flames and smoke, which blocked everyone's vision. When the smoke cleared, Wan Hu was gone!

THE V2 ROCKET, MADE BY THE GERMANS IN 1942, WAS THE FIRST ROCKET CAPABLE OF REACHING SPACE.

• FACT FILE •

In 1931 Johannes Winkler launched his HW-1 rocket. It went 1.9m (6ft) into the air, turned over and fell back to the ground.

WHAT IS A SPACE SHUTTLE?

The space shuttle is a spacecraft. It was developed to provide a reusable, and therefore cheaper, vehicle for launching satellites and for other work in space.

The shuttle itself is a bulky delta-winged aircraft with extremely powerful rocket motors. When it is launched, two solid-fuel booster rockets are strapped to its sides and a giant fuel tank is fixed to its belly. The rockets and fuel tank both fall away after the launch, and the rockets are recovered and then reused. When it is in orbit, the shuttle's cargo bay opens to release satellites or allow the crew to work in space. The shuttle lands on a runway just like a conventional aeroplane.

At takeoff the Space Shuttle weighs 2,000 tonnes. It burns almost all of its fuel in the first few minutes after launch, then continues to coast into its orbit 300km (185 miles) above the surface of the Earth.

FACT FILE

You cannot breathe in space because there is no air. Oxygen is the gas we need to stay alive, so all space missions carry their own air supply. When astronauts go on a 'space walk' they wear a spacesuit that provides them with the correct air and pressure.

WHAT ARE THE BENEFITS OF SPACE EXPLORATION?

Satellites can be used to perform all sorts of roles in communication, including mobile banking, vehicle navigation and weather monitoring.

Until 1957, human beings were just observers of the Solar System. Now they have entered the realm of space and gathered first-hand knowledge of their planetary environment. Twelve men have landed on the Moon, set up data-gathering experiments on the lunar surface and brought back lunar rocks and soil for study and analysis.

The hidden side of the Moon and the planets Mercury, Venus, Mars, Jupiter and Saturn have been photographed and studied. The Earth and its weather have been studied, and communication relays and navigational aids have also been established.

• FACT FILE •

Space telescopes are a revolutionary piece of equipment for astronomers and are able to focus on objects that are not visible to the human eye.

MACHINES AND TECHNOLOGY

CONTENTS

WHAT WERE THE FIRST CLOCKS LIKE?

The sundial was one of the earliest devices for measuring time. But it can work only on a day with plenty of sunlight. Early peoples also used ropes with knots tied at regular intervals. In the ninth century, candles were marked with spaced lines. When burned, such devices measured time, but this was not very accurate as a draught could cause the candle to burn more quickly.

An hourglass or sandglass tells time by means of sand trickling through a narrow opening. A water clock, or clepsydra, measures time by allowing water to drip slowly from one marked container into another. By the 1700s, people had developed clocks and watches that told time to the minute. Modern electronic and atomic clocks can measure time with far greater accuracy.

Candle clock

Sundial

?

DID YOU KNOW THAT THE OLDEST CLOCK IN THE WORLD IS IN ENGLAND? IT CAN BE FOUND IN THE AISLE OF SALISBURY CATHEDRAL AND DATES FROM AROUND 1386.

• FACT FILE •

The Sun was the first clock. Long ago people guessed at the time of day by watching the Sun as it moved across the sky. It was easy to recognize sunrise and sunset, but harder to know when it was noon, the time when the Sun is highest above the horizon.

WHERE WAS THE FIRST LOCK FOUND?

The oldest key-operated lock still in existence was found in the citadel of King Sargon II. The citadel was built in the Assyrian capital of Khorsabad in the late eighth century BCE.

Similar locks are shown in Egyptian art dating from about 2000 BCE. These large wooden locks had bolts with pegs that served as simple pin-tumblers. A matching wooden key raised the tumblers and released the bolt.

The ancient Romans developed the first warded locks, which remained the most common locks until the 19th century. These locks have several fixed ridges or obstacles called wards that stop the wrong key from operating the lock. The correct key has notches cut into it that match the wards inside the lock. When a person inserts the correct key, the key fits past the wards and moves a spring inside the lock. The spring is attached to a bolt or shackle – the curved part of a padlock that snaps into the padlock's body. When the spring moves, the bolt or shackle slides to a locked or unlocked position.

• FACT FILE •

Tumbler locks have movable metal parts called tumblers that prevent the wrong key from opening the lock. Because tumblers provide more security than wards, most door locks use some type of tumbler arrangement.

THERE ARE MANY TYPES OF LOCK. THE THREE MOST COMMON ARE LEVERS, DEADBOLTS AND PADLOCKS.

WHEN WERE FIREWORKS INTRODUCED?

Chinese crackers were probably the first fireworks to be made and this was about 2,000 years ago. They are still used in China and throughout the East to celebrate weddings, births and religious festivals. They are also used to scare away evil spirits. It is probable that gunpowder was developed in China because they used potassium nitrate (saltpeter) to cure their meat, and so it was readily available.

The earliest recorded use of gunpowder in England is by the Franciscan monk Roger Bacon (born 1214). He recorded his experiments with a mixture, which was very inadequate by today's standards but was recognizable as gunpowder. His formula contained charcoal and sulphur because there was no natural source of saltpeter available.

? DID YOU KNOW THAT GUNPOWDER HAS BEEN USED AS A CONDIMENT IN THE PAST? IT HAS ALSO BEEN USED AS A CURING AGENT FOR BACON AND HAM.

• FACT FILE •

In January 1606, in London, Parliament established 5 November as a day of public thanksgiving. The day, known as Guy Fawkes Day, is still celebrated with bonfires, fireworks and the carrying of 'guys' through the streets.

Fireworks have been used for centuries in ancient Indian and Siamese ceremonies.

WHEN WAS GUNPOWDER FIRST USED?

It was the Chinese who first started using gunpowder in warfare. By the year 1232, the Chinese had discovered black powder (gunpowder) and had learned to use it to make explosive bombs as well as propelling forces for rockets. Drawings made in military documents later show powder rockets tied to arrows and spears.

When the Mongols laid siege to the city of Kaifeng, the capital of Henan province, the Chinese defenders used weapons that were described as 'arrows of flying fire'. In the same battle, it is reported, the defenders dropped from the walls of the city a kind of bomb described as 'heaven-shaking thunder'.

In the same century rockets appeared in Europe. There is an indication that their first use was by the Mongols in the Battle of Legnica in 1241. The Arabs are also reported to have used rockets, in 1249.

• FACT FILE •

Guy Fawkes is best known for his efforts to blow up the Parliament building in London, in 1605. This became known as the 'Gunpowder Plot'. His plan, however, was foiled.

HOW CAN LEVERS BE USEFUL?

For thousands of years people have used levers as a way of transferring a force from one place to another, and to change the amount of movement that results. Levers are really useful when you need to move a heavy object without the use of machinery.

To move a heavy object, a long lever can help. The lever is free to move about a point called the fulcrum. The shorter end of the lever is placed under the object, and force is applied to the longer end. This will cause the object to be lifted, but the long end of the lever will have to be pushed down a long way to lift the object only a short distance. For example, with a long-enough lever you could lift a car for a short distance.

HOW A LEVER WORKS

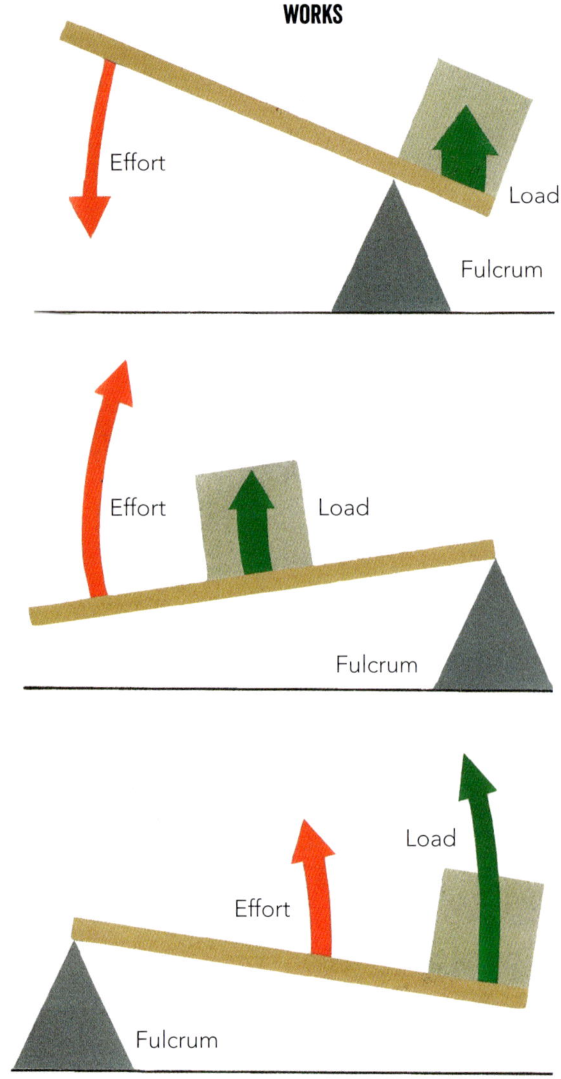

• FACT FILE •

Scissors work with a lever action. The cutting blades are worked by putting your forefinger and thumb into the holes in the handles and pushing together.

WHAT ARE GEARS?

A gear is a mechanical device that transfers rotating motion and power from one part of a machine to another. Gears are produced in a wide range of sizes, and they vary greatly in use. They range from the tiny gears that drive the hands of a watch to the huge gears that turn the propeller of a supertanker. A simple gear consists of a metal wheel or disc with slots called teeth around the edge. Gears always work in pairs. The teeth of one gear mesh (fit together) with the teeth of the other gear. Each gear has a metal axle in the middle. The axle of one gear is connected to a power source, such as an electric motor. When the power axle turns, its gear turns and causes the second gear to rotate in the opposite direction. This action powers the axle of the second gear to do useful work.

• FACT FILE •

A bicycle's gear system makes pedalling easier at certain times. Low gears, which make it easy to pedal up hills or against the wind, rotate the rear wheel only a little bit during each turn of the pedals.

Many mechanical pieces have gears – from watches to bicycles to cars.

WHAT IS THE METRIC SYSTEM?

The most widely used system of weights and measures is the metric system, which was devised by a committee of French scientists in 1791. Measures of length include centimetres (cm), metres (m) and kilometres (km); among those for volume are millilitre (ml), centilitre (cl) and litre (l) and for weight milligrams (mg), grams (g), kilograms (kg) and tonnes (T). Area is measured in metres squared (m^2) and hectares (ha) and temperatures in degrees centigrade (°C), in which water freezes at 0°C and boils at 100°C. The measurements are all interlinked: under the correction conditions of temperature and pressure, 1 litre of water weighs 1 kilogram and 1 millilitre (also sometimes called a cubic centimetre) weighs 1 milligram.

• FACT FILE •

TEMPERATURE

°C	0	20	40	60	80	100
°F	32	68	104	140	176	212

SPEED

Kmh	20	30	40	50	60	70
Mph	13	19	25	31	37	43

WEIGHT

Kg	10	20	30	40	50	60
Stones	2.8	5.5	8.3	11	13.7	16.5

LENGTH

M	1	2	3	4	5
Ft	3.3	6.6	9.8	13.1	16.4

WHY DO WE NEED NUMBERS?

Numbers are used to describe the amount of things. We can express numbers in words, by hand gestures or in writing, using symbols or numerals. When we talk about a number we use words (five) rather than the figure (5), but when we write, we use both words and figures. Numbers can describe how many objects there are, or their position among lots of objects – for example, 1st or 5th.

Other types of numbers describe how many units of something there are, for example how many kilograms/pounds (weight) or metres/feet (length). Numbers are just a convenient way of describing ideas.

• FACT FILE •

Roman numerals are still used today for certain purposes. They appear on some watch and clock faces and when numbers have a certain importance, such as in the title of a monarch.

I	1	VIII	8
II	2	IX	9
III	3	X	10
IV	4	XX	20
V	5	L	50
VI	6	C	100
VII	7	M	1,000

HOW IS AN ELECTROMAGNET MADE?

Electromagnets can only produce magnetism when an electrical current passes through them. They usually consist of a metal core made of iron or similar material, around which are wrapped many coils of thin insulated wire. The metal core becomes magnetized when an electric current passes through the wire coil, but the effect disappears immediately the current is shut off. Very powerful electromagnets can be made by using many coils and strong electrical currents.

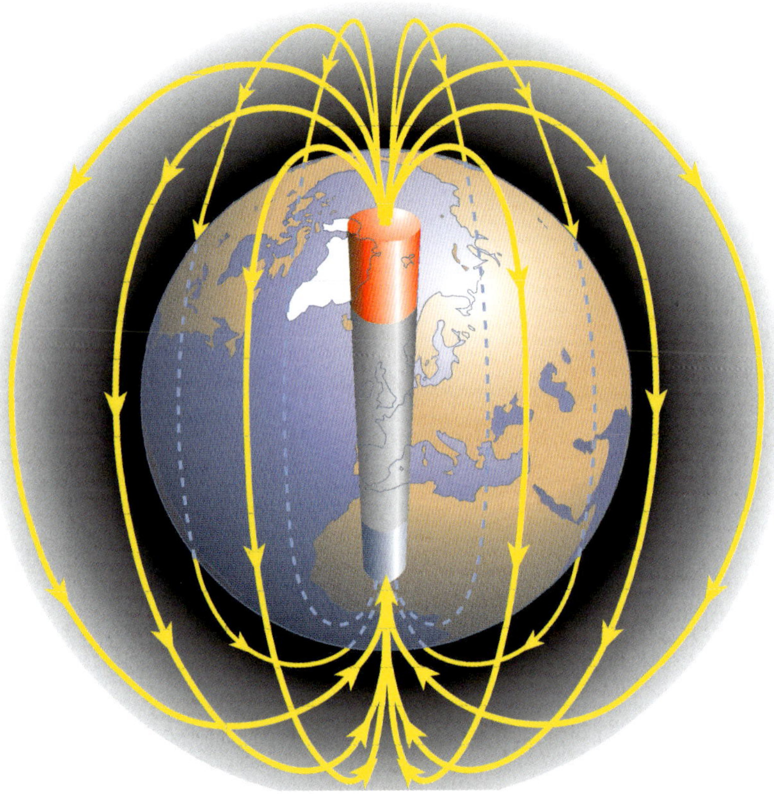

The Earth is just like a magnet. Lines of force run from the north to the south magnetic poles and a compass can detect these.

• FACT FILE •

One of the most important uses of magnets is in electric motors, which power many machines, ranging from small toys to enormous railway engines. The Japanese Maglev train uses powerful electromagnets to levitate above the track.

WHERE WOULD YOU FIND A TRANSISTOR?

A transistor has two basic functions: (1) to switch electric current on and off and (2) to amplify or strengthen electric current.

A transistor is a tiny device that controls the flow of electric current and is found in radios, television sets, computers and almost every other kind of electronic equipment. Transistors vary in size tremendously.

Transistors replaced electronic components called vacuum tubes almost completely in the 1950s and 1960s because they have a number of advantages over vacuum tubes. For example, transistors are smaller, lighter, less expensive to produce, cheaper to operate, and more reliable than vacuum tubes.

Transistors are the main components built into computer chips. Some chips are no larger than a fingernail, yet contain millions of transistors.

• FACT FILE •

The ability to amplify signals makes transistors essential parts of radios and television sets. The broadcast waves that travel through the air generate weak currents in a radio or TV antenna. Transistors amplify these signals to produce sounds and pictures.

HOW DOES AN ELECTRIC LIGHT WORK?

In 1800, Humphrey Davy connected wires to the ends of a weak battery and attached a piece of carbon to each of the free ends of the wires. By touching the two pieces of carbon together and drawing them slightly apart, he produced an 'electric arc', proving that electric light was possible, but the source of the electricity was not strong enough.

In a traditional light bulb, a current is passed through a very thin filament of metal with a high resistance to its flow, which becomes white-hot and produces light. The bulb contains an inert gas so the filament won't burn.

The glass tubes in low-energy bulbs are filled with mercury vapour and electronic ballast, through which electricity flows causing the mercury vapour to give off light in the ultraviolet range. This stimulates the phosphorous coating on the inside the glass tubes to produce light.

• FACT FILE •

Lightning is actually electricity. A huge electrical charge can be built up in certain weather conditions, and this leads to thunderstorms when a bolt of lightning leaps between the Earth and a cloud. The air is heated to a very high temperature, causing the explosive noise of thunder as it suddenly expands.

HOW DOES AN ELECTRIC MOTOR WORK?

Most powered devices in the home contain an electric motor, which turns electric energy into movement. When an electric current passes along a wire in the field of a magnet, it exerts a force to move the wire. Usually the magnet is still, while the coil carrying the current spins round inside it.

Domestic motors run on alternating current, and the current in the coil is rapidly reversed so the magnet's poles change direction, forcing the coil to make another half-turn. This process is repeated very rapidly as the motor turns.

When a motor runs from a direct current, which flows in only one direction, a device called a commutator reverses the current and causes the coil to rotate. It is this motion that can be used to drive a huge number of machines, such as washing machines, hairdryers and food processors to name but a few.

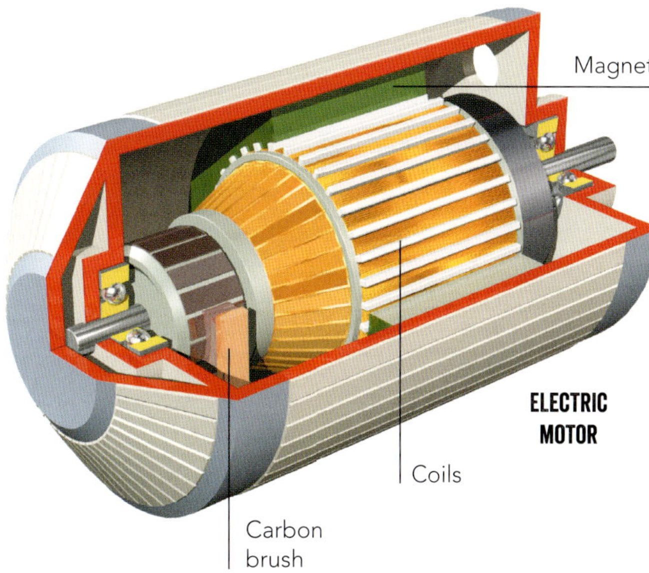

ELECTRIC MOTOR

• FACT FILE •

A digital multimeter measures voltage, among other things. An electrical current flows from an area with high to low electrical potential, as in one battery terminal to another. The difference between the two is then measured in volts (V).

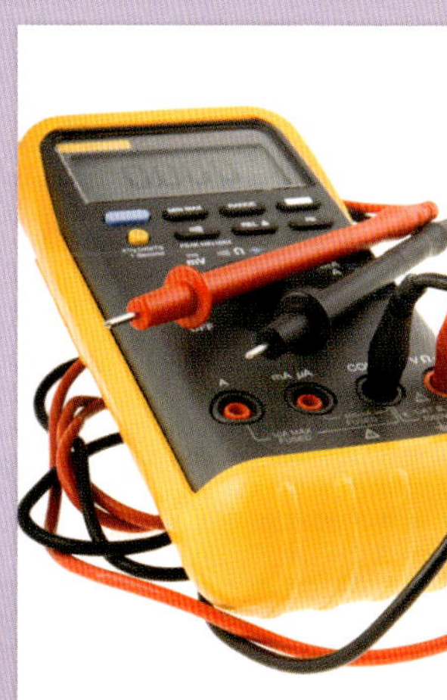

WHY DO WE USE CIRCUIT BOARDS?

Any modern electrical device requires a huge number of connections to join together all the small components needed for it to work effectively. At one time these connections were made by wires that had to be soldered together. The wires have now been replaced by the printed circuit board, which is effectively a picture of the wiring that works just as well.

The image is literally photographed onto a special board, which is covered with a thin layer of copper. Chemicals are used to dissolve most of the copper leaving behind a thin film of metal bands to which all the components can be attached. Circuit boards are very light, compact and inexpensive to make.

PRINTED CIRCUIT BOARD TECHNOLOGY IS CONSTANTLY CHANGING. BOARDS ARE GETTING SMALLER AND SMALLER AND SCIENTISTS ARE NOW WORKING ON VERSIONS THAT ARE BIODEGRADABLE.

• FACT FILE •

Appliances containing electronic circuits can perform very complicated tasks and even appear to think for themselves. A good example of this is a personal computer.

WHICH RADIO RUNS WITHOUT ELECTRICITY?

This emergency weather radio can be powered by batteries, solar or hand crank.

In 1991, British inventor Trevor Baylis invented a portable wind-up radio, enabling millions in the developing world, with no permanent electricity supply, to receive broadcasts. The radio works, not on electricity, but by winding up a spring, which slowly uncoils and powers a small generator.

The portable radio was invented in 1947. The invention was made possible by the development of a device called a transistor, which replaced the valves inside radios that picked up radio signals. Transistors were much smaller than valves, so it now became possible to make lighter weight, portable radios.

In 1955 a Japanese company called Tokyo Tsushin Kogyo decided to build a portable radio for the US market. Before they began to sell the radio, they changed the company name to something Americans could say easily – the new company name was Sony.

• FACT FILE •

On 18 October 1954 the world's 'first pocket radio' went on sale. The Regency TR1 is just 12 cm (4¾ in) high. Around 100,000 TR1s sold during the radio's only year of production.

WHERE DOES THE WORD 'RADAR' COME FROM?

Radar is a scientific method used to detect and locate moving or fixed objects. Radar can determine the direction, distance, height and speed of objects that are much too far away for the human eye to see. It can find objects as small as insects or as large as mountains. Radar can even operate well at night and in heavy fog, rain or snow.

Almost every radar set works by sending radio waves towards an object and receiving the waves that are reflected from the object. The time it takes for the reflected waves to return indicates the object's range – how far away it is. The direction from which the reflected waves return shows the object's location.

• FACT FILE •

Radar uses microwave radiation to detect distant objects. The microwaves usually scan round in a circle, and the echoes sent back produce an image on a screen.

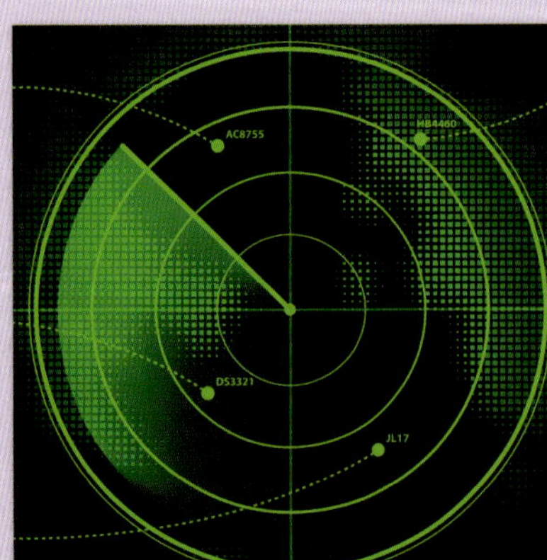

THE WORD 'RADAR' COMES FROM RADIO DETECTION AND RANGING.

WHICH BEAM OF LIGHT CAN CUT METAL?

THE WORD LASER STANDS FOR LIGHT AMPLIFICATION BY STIMULATED EMISSION OF RADIATION.

When used as a laser, it is possible for a narrow beam of extremely strong light to cut metal. The first laser was built in 1960 by scientist Theodore Maiman, who used a rod-shaped crystal of synthetic ruby to produce a very bright, very narrow beam of light. Lasers amplify light by causing photons to be bounced back and forth in a substance (which can be solid, liquid or gas), which add extra energy. The result is that intense light is emitted in a very narrow beam.

The intense beam of light produced by a laser can be used to produce images for publicity or entertainment purposes. Lasers are also used to cut metal, and for precision cuts in operations. In CD players, laser light is scanned across the CD's silvery surface, reading the tiny changes in light reflected back. They are also used in office printers and scanners. In engineering, the intense narrow beam of light is used to measure and align roads and tunnels.

• FACT FILE •

Lasers are used every day in our shops and banks to scan banknotes to see whether they are forgeries. This is done by passing the note under an ultraviolet light scanner.

WHEN WAS THE TELESCOPE INVENTED?

Galileo is credited with having developed telescopes for astronomical observation in 1609. While the largest of his telescopes was only about 120cm (47in) long and had an objective diameter of 5cm (2in), it was equipped with an eyepiece that provided an upright image.

Galileo used his modest apparatus to explore the valleys and mountains of the Moon, the phases of Venus, and the four largest satellites, which had never been systematically observed before.

The reflecting telescope was developed in 1668 by Newton. He became the first person to use a telescope to see the moons orbiting the planet Jupiter. He also used his theories about gravity to show why the planets orbit the Sun.

• FACT FILE •

Special solar telescopes have been constructed so that the intensity of the image of the Sun or other planets, will not damage the observer's eye.

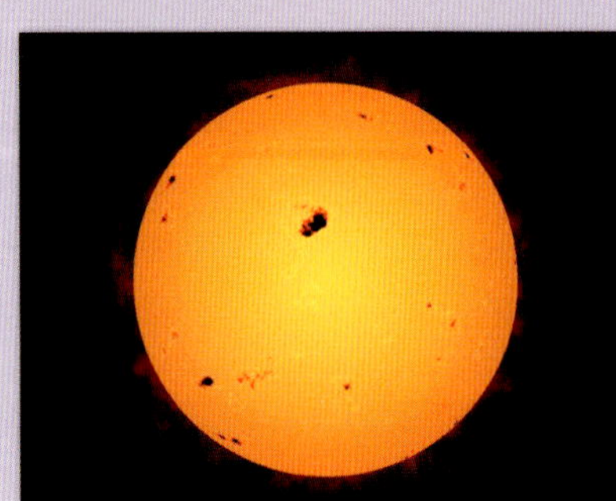

WHERE WOULD YOU FIND A PERISCOPE?

Periscopes are most commonly associated with submarines, but they can also be used by tanks, military helicopters and individuals.

The simplest version is a tube with one opening at the top front and another at the bottom rear. Inside are two mirrors, set at a 45-degree angle to the tube and parallel to each other. An image of what the top opening of the periscope is pointed at is reflected from the top mirror down to the bottom mirror and then out of the lower opening so that the viewer can see it. In a battle, this allows the viewer to see over the top of walls or trees so he can shoot at the opposition without exposing himself to their fire. This simple sort of periscope was used in the trenches in northern Europe in World War I.

Submarine periscopes are more complicated as they have prisms instead of mirrors and lenses that magnify the image. Some modern submarines use electronic imaging techniques today, instead of mechanical periscopes.

• FACT FILE •

The armed forces also use helicopters to observe the movements of enemy troops and ships. Many naval helicopters have devices to locate and track submarines.

WHY ARE BLAST FURNACES USED?

Iron is the most widely used of all metals. It is cheap and very strong, so it can be used to make the supports for huge buildings and bridges. Smelting is what is known as a reduction reaction. It is a method of extracting iron from iron ore. The process of smelting takes place in something called a blast furnace, as pictured left. The blast furnace gets its name from the hot air that is blasted into it. This is where iron ore, limestone and coke (a form of carbon) are heated together while hot air is blasted into the furnace. The carbon in the coke reacts with the oxygen in the air to form carbon monoxide. This in turn takes oxygen from the iron ore, leaving behind iron mixed with a little carbon.

• FACT FILE •

Alloys of steel, in which steel is combined with other metals, can be very useful. Railway tracks are made of an alloy of steel and manganese.

THE TEMPERATURE INSIDE A BLAST FURNACE REACHES 2,000°C (3632°F).

WHEN DID THE CANNING OF FOOD AND DRINK FIRST START?

People had been trying for thousands of years to find better ways to preserve food for a long time. The first patent for a 'tin canister' for preserving food was granted in England to Peter Durand in 1810. He got the idea from the canisters in which tea was packed. In America, the name became shortened to 'tin can', and the industry was called 'canning', while in England it is known as 'tinning'.

The first cannery in the United States was one for fish, and was started by Ezra Dagget in New York City in 1819. The next year, fruit preserves and tomatoes were stored in glass in Boston.

To can a food successfully, it must be heated at a high enough temperature to kill the organisms (moulds, yeasts, bacteria) that may cause fresh food to spoil; the tin can or glass jar must be free from germs and it must be sealed air-tight.

• FACT FILE •

In 1810 the French chef called Nicholas Appert discovered a way of preserving food by packing food into wide-mouth bottles. He sealed the bottles and then lowered them into a boiler filled with hot water. A lid was put on, so that the bottles would heat in their boiling water bath. Some foods, fruit and vegetables in particular, may also be preserved by pickling then stored in jars.

WHEN IS A BAROMETER USED?

A barometer is used to measure the changes in air pressure.

Air pressure varies across different parts of the Earth's surface, and these differences cause winds. Air moves from an area of high pressure, or an anticyclone, to an area of low pressure, or a depression. Depressions are usually associated with worsening weather conditions and rain. In a mercury barometer the air pressure pushes down on the mercury, which is forced up the barometer to give an accurate reading.

Air pressure is greatest at sea level, where it amounts to 6.7kg per 2.5cm^2 (14.7lb per 1in^2). It is greatest there because that is the bottom of the atmosphere. At higher altitudes the pressure is less.

• FACT FILE •

The higher we go the less air pressure there is. This is the reason that spacesuits and the cabins of high-flying planes are pressurized. They are designed to maintain the air pressure our bodies must have.

WHEN DID WEATHER FORECASTING BEGIN?

Warm front

People have been able to forecast the weather for hundreds of years. Meteorologists have used simple instruments like thermometers, rain gauges, barometers and wind gauges for many years, but with the advent of satellite photography, weather forecasting has been transformed. With the use of computers, increasingly accurate forecasting is now possible.

Traditional forecasters have been known to use pine cones, which open and close according to the humidity of the air. An open cone is supposed to mean dry weather. Seaweed also responds to changes in humidity. Dry seaweed indicates dry weather.

• FACT FILE •

There is an old saying regarding the weather: If the oak tree has its leaves before the ash then it will be a fine summer.

WHAT IS A GEOSTATIONARY SATELLITE?

Satellite's view of Earth

• FACT FILE •

Satellites also carry search-and-rescue transmission instruments so that pilots and mariners in distress can relay messages through them for help.

There are two types of weather satellite for long- and short-term observations, which together give a complete picture of Earth's weather system. Geostationary operational, environmental satellites (GOES) remain in orbit 36,000 km (22,370 miles) above the Equator, giving detailed, constant and accurate information about the movement of storms, hurricanes, thunderstorms and other severe weather patterns as quickly as possible, with the help of radar and other ground systems. Polar, orbiting environmental satellites (POES) orbit much closer to the Earth's surface and offer visible infrared photos that measure moisture and temperature, tracking weather patterns and climate.

WHEN WAS THE FIRST WEATHER SATELLITE LAUNCHED?

Forty years ago, weather predictions were about as accurate as forecasts of who will win the lottery. In the days before television could warn on a Wednesday of rainy periods at the weekend, weather monitoring was limited to wind, temperature and rainfall gauges aboard aeroplanes, balloons and ships.

All that changed on 1 April, 1960 when the US Government launched the first weather satellite, called TIROS 1, into the Earth's orbit from Cape Canaveral, Florida. It paved the way for generations of weather satellites that today help with everything from monitoring crops to tracking the movement of mosquitoes across continents.

WHEN THE INFORMATION FROM THE GOES AND POES IS COMBINED, IT TAKES ONLY SIX HOURS TO PROVIDE A COMPLETE PICTURE OF WEATHER CONDITIONS ACROSS THE ENTIRE SURFACE OF THE EARTH.

• FACT FILE •

Thanks to the Internet, meteorologists can view high-resolution satellite images of incoming storms, allowing coastal areas enough advance warning to evacuate.

WHERE WOULD YOU FIND A WELL?

Spring water is usually free from pollutants, and often contains minerals from the rock through which it has travelled. We call this mineral water.

In some areas of the world there is no piped and purified water supply, either because it is too remote an area or, because it is too expensive. Here, people rely on wells for drinking water. The simplest well is just a hole in the ground, lined with bricks or stone, sunk deep enough to reach the natural level of the underlying water – the water table. Water is drawn up by hand or pumped to the surface. An artesian well is sunk deeper into a layer of porous water-bearing rock (an aquifer) that lies between two layers of rock that water cannot pass through (impermeable rock). If the well is sunk into the low-lying layer of porous rock, natural water pressure will force the water up the well shaft. If the pressure is insufficient, it will need to be pumped or hauled up. Springs occur naturally where the end of an aquifer reaches the ground's surface.

• FACT FILE •

Niagara Falls is one of the most spectacular natural wonders of North America. The energy of the crashing water at the falls has been used since 1891 to generate electricity.

WHERE IS THE THAMES BARRIER?

The Thames Barrier is in East London, near Greenwich. It was opened in 1982. It is needed because there is an increased risk of flooding. London is sinking into the clay on which it is built, and because northern Britain is rising as it recovers from the weight of ice that covered it in the last Ice Age, the southeast of Britain is tilting downwards.

Thirdly, and most worryingly, climate change is melting the ice caps and leading to a rise in sea levels. If a high tide occurred at the same time as a bad storm, which would also raise sea levels, without the barrier a flood could destroy large parts of London.

• FACT FILE •

Floods can also occur inland, when heavy rain drains off the land and causes rivers to burst their banks. This effect is made worse in built-up areas where the rain cannot soak into the ground.

WHEN WAS THE TELEVISION INVENTED?

The television was not 'invented' at one particular time by one particular person. The processes that enable a television to operate were developed over a period of time.

In 1875, G. R. Carey made the first basic television system using photoelectric cells. An object was focused through a lens onto a bank of photoelectric cells. Each cell controlled how much electricity would be passed on to a light bulb. Crude outlines of the object then appeared in lights.

In 1923 the first-ever practical transmission of pictures over wires was achieved. There was also a great development in television camera technology. The television as we know it today had been fully developed by 1945.

Twenty-first century technology has brought high-definition digital television and flat screen interactive television sets, with hundreds of satellite channels.

• FACT FILE •

The first television sets transmitted programmes in black and white. It wasn't until the 1970s that colour TV became widespread. Remote controls first arrived in the 1980s.

WHEN WAS THE INTERNET STARTED?

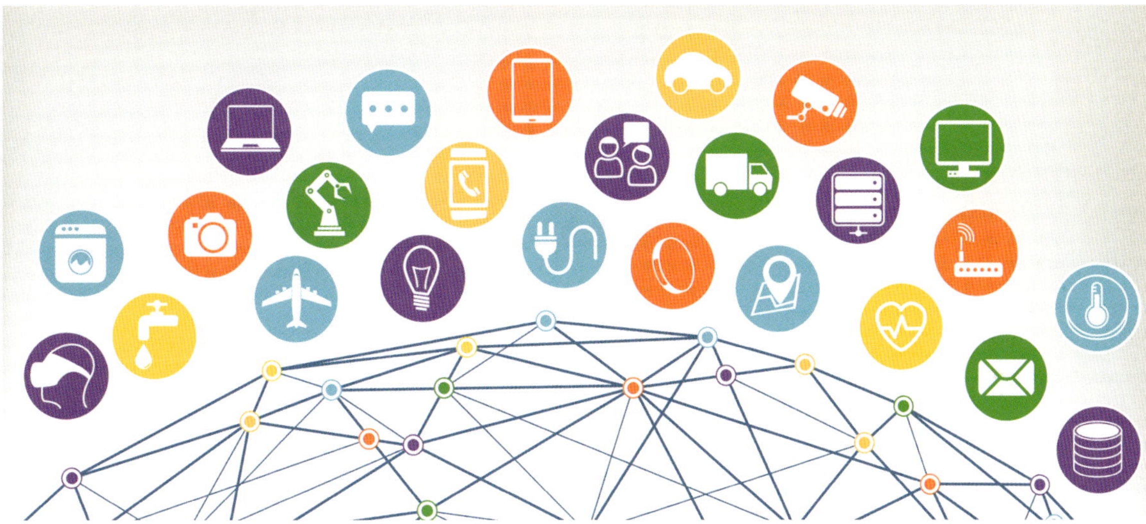

The Internet was created in 1983. The idea behind the Internet came from the US Defence department who had a basic version of the Internet set up as a secure system for their information.

The Internet was born from a fundamentally academic origin, as a framework connecting numerous computer networks together. It has rapidly developed into a very popular commercial medium. By the mid-1990s, millions of computers all around the world were connected on the 'world wide web'.

The limits of technology are always changing, and the Internet tests the capabilities of modern developments to the full.

• FACT FILE •

Modern communications have affected our lives in many ways. Since the 1980s the mobile phone has proved to be the most popular means of communication. It was publicly introduced in Chicago in 1983 and was a success from the start.

WHERE WAS THE FIRST SKYSCRAPER?

The first 'skyscraper' described in writing was probably the Tower of Babel, a possible seven-storey Babylonian ziggurat depicted in the Bible (Genesis). It was built by the descendents of Noah on the plain of Shinar, in an attempt to reach the heavens and be nearer to God.

In the Middle Ages, European architects designed cathedrals with tall towers and soaring spires with the same intention. The tallest spire in England can be seen on Salisbury cathedral, completed in 1320, rising to a height of 123m (404ft) above ground level.

• FACT FILE •

In 1889 the Eiffel Tower in Paris was the world's tallest structure rising 300 m (984 ft) above the city.

In the early 20th century, architects in New York competed to build the tallest skyscraper, a record held for many years by the Empire State Building (1930).

HOW IS SOUND PUT ON A CD?

CD-Roms hold data, sound files and pictures; DVDs and Blu-rays have replaced video cassettes as a way of playing back movies.

Compact discs (CDs), CD-Roms, digital video discs (DVDs) and minidiscs are all made of a thin layer of metal, usually aluminium, covered in a protective coating of clear, hard plastic. In the case of CDs, sound is translated into electronic signals that are then converted into a digital format. This is impressed into the metal of the disc as a series of millions of tiny pits. During playback, a laser reads the changes in the metal and translates these back into sound.

In the same way that the advent of the CD ousted vinyl singles and albums, improved technology that has led to increased storage capacity on hand-held players, downloading music files from the Internet straight to these devices, as well as illegal file-sharing, have led to dramatic reductions in the number of CDs sold.

• FACT FILE •

Frequency modulation, usually simply called FM, is a method of sending sound signals on radio waves. Amplitude modulation (AM) and FM are the two chief means of transmitting music and speech, although digital technology is increasing in popularity.

WHAT IS MRI?

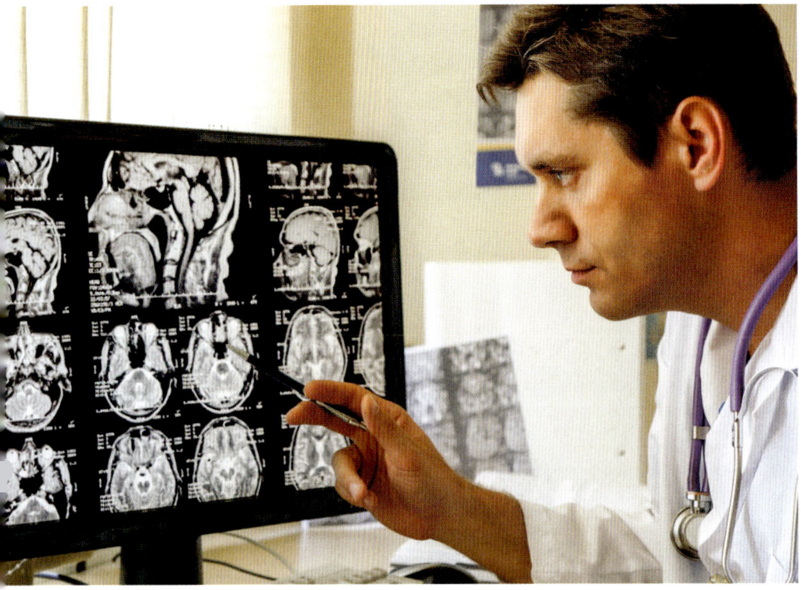

Magnetic resonance imaging (or MRI) is a technique used in medicine for producing images of tissues inside the body. Physicians use these images to diagnose certain diseases, disorders and injuries. MRI is an important diagnostic tool because it enables doctors to identify abnormal tissue without having to open the body through surgery. MRI does not expose the patient to radiation, unlike tests that use X-rays. MRI uses a very powerful magnet and therefore cannot be used on people with metal implants, such as pacemakers or artificial joints.

MRI SCANNERS ARE USED TO DETECT BONE FRACTURES THAT ARE TOO SMALL TO BE SEEN ON AN X-RAY. THEY ALSO REVEAL ELECTRICAL ACTIVITY IN THE BRAIN.

FACT FILE

An exciting area of medicine is the Human Genome Project. Its aim is to identify all the 100,000 genes in the human body by studying DNA. This project involves the co-operation of 18 different countries.

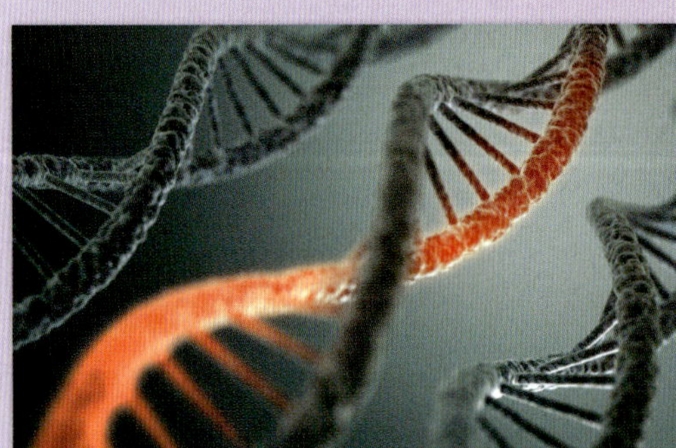

WHAT IS A PATENT?

A patent is an agreement between an inventor and the government that no-one else can use his invention without his permission for a given period of years. The inventor files his design at the patent office when he applies for the patent. If a patent is granted, it ensures that the inventor earns the reward of profits for his invention, but once the period of the agreement, which varies from country to country, has finished, the design is available for other people to use. Nowadays, patents are extremely important for such manufacturing fields as medicine and for computer software, which can generate millions of dollars of profit. If a patent-holder discovers that another person or company has breached the patent by using the invention or incorporated it into another invention, he or she may claim damages for loss of potential profit.

If an idea is not new – or useful – a patent may not be granted.

• FACT FILE •

Like breach of copyright, breach of patent is called piracy. Some countries' governments are not as stringent as others about punishing breaches of patents and as a result, cheaper pirate versions of inventions are made.

SPACE EXPLORATION

CONTENTS

WHAT WAS THE BIG BANG?

Nobody knows how the Universe began, but the most common theory is the Big Bang. According to this theory, the Universe was formed from an immense explosion 13 billion years ago. Before the Big Bang, everything in the Universe was packed into a tiny area, smaller than the nucleus of an atom. This point was called a 'singularity' and was incredibly hot. It was released in an explosion so powerful that all of the matter in the singularity was blasted into an area larger than a galaxy in less than a fraction of a second. There is very strong evidence to support the theory of the Big Bang. The strongest 'proof' is a weak signal that has been detected in space. This is thought to be an echo from the energy released by the force of the Big Bang.

The idea of the Big Bang has been around since 1922, but was not considered seriously until the 1940s.

• FACT FILE •

According to ancient Egyptian mythology, the fundamentals of life – air (Shu) and moisture (Tefnut) – came from the spittle of their Sun God Re. From the union of Shu and Tefnut came Geb, the Earth god, and Nut, the sky goddess. The first human beings were born from Re's tears.

WHAT IS THE UNIVERSE MADE UP OF?

The Universe is everything and anything that exists. The Universe is still a mystery to scientists. It is made up almost entirely of hydrogen and helium. These are the two lightest elements. All the rest of the matter in the Universe is very rare.

Elements such as silicon, carbon and others are concentrated into clouds, stars and planets. The Universe is held together by four invisible forces. Gravity and electromagnetism are the two familiar forces. The other two kinds are strong and weak nuclear forces. These operate only inside the incredibly tiny nuclei of atoms, holding the tiny particles together.

PLANET EARTH IS AROUND 4.54 BILLION YEARS OLD, BUT LIFE ON EARTH IS REALLY VERY RECENT – RELATIVELY.

• FACT FILE •

The large Hadron Collider, successfully tested in 2010 is teaching us more about particle acceleration and the birth of stars and the deepest laws of nature.

WHAT IS THE MILKY WAY?

There are at least 3,000,000,000 stars in the galaxy.

There is probably nothing more mysterious and wonderful looking in the sky than the Milky Way, stretching like a band of jewels from one end of the sky to the other. In early Christian times, people thought it was a pathway for the angels, so they could go up to heaven on it. But today we know the real facts about the Milky Way.

Our galaxy is shaped roughly like a watch – round and flat. If you could get above it and look down on it, it would look like an immense watchface. But we are inside the galaxy, and when we look up we are looking towards the edge from inside the 'watch'. So we see that edge curving around us. As there are millions of stars in it, we see it as the Milky Way.

• FACT FILE •

It takes eight minutes for light from the Sun to reach the Earth. For light from the middle of the galaxy to reach the Sun, it takes about 27,000 years.

?

DID YOU KNOW THAT PLUTO USED TO BE CONSIDERED A PLANET? IN 2009 IT WAS RECLASSIFIED AS A DWARF PLANET.

WHAT ARE THE PLANETS OF THE SOLAR SYSTEM?

The four planets that are nearest to the Sun are called the inner planets. In order from the Sun, they are Mercury, Venus, Earth and Mars. The inner planets are different from the outer planets, which are further away from the Sun, because they are made of rock. Each of the inner planets has an atmosphere. However, apart from the Earth, the atmospheres of the inner planets are very thin and would be poisonous to humans. The outer planets, which are Jupiter, Saturn, Uranus, and Neptune are composed mainly of frozen gases, and are large but light.

• FACT FILE •

Science fiction writers thought that life might exist beneath the thick clouds of Venus. We now know that conditions there are too extreme for life as we know it.

WHAT DOES EARTH LOOK LIKE FROM SPACE?

Earth is designated in astronomy as the third planet outward from the Sun. Its single most outstanding feature is that its near-surface environments are the only places in the Universe known to maintain life.

Those who have gone into space have come back with a changed perspective and reverence for the planet Earth. The effect from space is obvious. One astronaut said after his trip, 'My first view – a panorama of brilliant deep blue ocean, shot with shades of green and grey and white – was of atolls and clouds'.

• FACT FILE •

Pioneer 10 was the first man-made object to leave the Solar System. It carried messages about life on Earth to be read by any extraterrestrial travellers who might meet the probe.

?

DID YOU KNOW THAT WE SENT MEN TO THE MOON BEFORE WE EXPLORED OUR DEEPEST OCEAN? NEIL ARMSTRONG AND BUZZ ALDRIN LANDED ON THE MOON IN 1969, WHILE DIVERS DIDN'T EXPLORE THE MID-ATLANTIC RIDGE UNTIL 1973.

HOW LONG DOES SUNLIGHT TAKE TO REACH EARTH?

From Earth the Sun looks small, because it is so far away. Light from the Sun takes about eight minutes to reach Earth. This light is still strong enough when it reaches the planet, however, to damage human eyes when viewed directly. The Sun's nearest stellar neighbour, Proxima Centauri, is 4.3 light-years from our Solar System, meaning that light from Proxima Centauri takes 4.3 years to reach the Sun. The Sun is so much closer to Earth than all other stars, that the intense light of the Sun keeps us from seeing any other stars during the daytime.

THE AVERAGE DISTANCE OF THE SUN FROM EARTH IS 150 MILLION KM (93 MILLION MILES).

• FACT FILE •

Did you know that in northern Scandinavia it doesn't get dark at all in the middle of summer? At the height of summer the tilt of the Earth causes northern countries to get more of the Sun's light.

WHAT IS ON THE FAR SIDE OF THE MOON?

The side of the Moon not visible from Earth is called the far side. It was first photographed by the Soviet *Lunar 3* probe in 1959 and was directly observed when the US *Apollo 8* mission orbited the Moon in 1968.

The far and near sides were seen to be very different in appearance. The far side is battered and densely cratered but has a much lower percentage of maria than the near side; 2.5% of the surface as opposed to 31.2%. The maria are huge impact craters that were later flooded by molten lava. Scientists speculate that the difference is due to a lower concentration of heat-producing elements on the far side. This is evident on geochemical maps produced from data provided by the Lunar Prospector gamma-ray spectrometer.

There are still many things we don't know about our Moon.

• FACT FILE •

Mountain ranges, thousands of metres high, form the walls of huge craters on the Moon's surface. Craters discovered on the near side of the Moon have been named after famous people.

WHY DOES THE MOON APPEAR TO CHANGE SHAPE?

Each month it seems as though the Moon changes shape. Of course, that is not really the case. Only the part of the Moon that is both turned towards the Earth and lit by the Sun is visible from Earth. The Moon orbits the Earth once every 27.3 days, a lunar month. As the Moon also takes exactly 27.3 days to turn on its axis, the same side of the Moon is always turned towards the Earth. The amount of the Moon that can be seen changes as the Moon's position changes. It is this change in the amount of the Moon's face, which we can see from Earth, that makes the Moon look as though it is changing shape.

• FACT FILE •

The Moon is close enough to us to have a tremendous effect on conditions on Earth. It is the pull of the Moon's gravity that causes tides in the seas.

?

DID YOU KNOW THAT OUR WORD 'MONTH' COMES FROM 'MOON'? DESPITE THIS, OUR CALENDAR MONTHS ARE NO LONGER LINKED TO THE PHASES OF THE MOON.

HOW LONG IS A MARTIAN DAY?

Mars is named after the Roman god of war because it appears fiery red in Earth's night sky.

The Martian day, or the time it takes Mars to rotate once on its axis, is about half an hour longer than an Earth day. Its year, or the time it takes to revolve once around the Sun, is about two Earth years long.

Mars is a relatively small planet, about half the diameter of the Earth and about one-tenth of Earth's mass. Because of the relative movements of the Earth and Mars around the Sun, Mars appears to move backwards in the sky for a short time when the two planets are closest.

FACT FILE

The surface of Mars is covered by a stony desert that contains lots of iron oxide, giving the planet its rusty-red appearance.

WHICH PLANET IS CALLED THE MORNING STAR?

Except for the Sun and the Moon, Venus is the brightest object in the sky. The planet is called the 'morning star' when it appears in the east at sunrise, and the 'evening star' when it is in the west at sunset.

Because of the distances of the orbits of Venus and Earth from the Sun, Venus is never visible more than three hours before sunrise or three hours after sunset. Venus's complete cloud cover and deep atmosphere make it difficult to study from Earth, and most of our knowledge of the planet has been obtained through the use of space vehicles, particularly those carrying probes that descend through the atmosphere.

IN ANCIENT TIMES THE EVENING STAR WAS CALLED HESPERUS AND THE MORNING STAR PHOSPHORUS OR LUCIFER.

• FACT FILE •

The powerful radar aboard the Magellan spacecraft has revealed huge active volcanoes, large solidified lava flows and a vast array of meteorite craters on the surface of Venus.

WHICH PLANET HAS THE GREATEST TEMPERATURE RANGE?

Mercury is only about one-third the size of the Earth. Mercury is very close to the Sun and has no substantial atmosphere. These factors contribute to the fact that the surface of Mercury has the greatest temperature range of any planet or natural satellite in our Solar System.

The surface temperature on the side of Mercury closest to the Sun reaches 427°C (800°F) – hot enough to melt tin. On the side facing away from the Sun, or the night side, the temperature drops to –183°C (–297°F). Mercury's atmosphere is very thin and is composed of helium and sodium. The surface of Mercury has been shaped by three processes: impact cratering where large objects struck the surface resulting in crater formation, volcanism where lava flooded the surface, and tectonic activity where the planet's crust moved in order to adjust to the planetary cooling and contracting.

Mercury is smaller than any other planet and has no satellites.

• FACT FILE •

Mercury has a large iron core which is between 1,800 and 1,900km (1,118 and 1,181 miles) thick. The outer shell is about 500km (311 miles) thick.

WHAT ARE THE RINGS OF SATURN?

Recently, space probes discovered that some of Saturn's rings are braided or twisted.

Shining rings of billions of tiny chips of ice, rock and dust surround Saturn. The rings reflect light strongly and can be clearly seen through a telescope from the Earth.

It was first thought that Saturn had three wide rings, but it is now known that the rings are actually made up of thousands of narrow ringlets. The rings are only 100m (328ft) thick, but they extend into space for 76,000km (47 miles).

The material in the rings was probably captured by Saturn's gravity when the Solar System was forming, or it might be the remains of a moon that has broken up.

• FACT FILE •

Pluto lies on the edge of deep space. It was only discovered in 1930, as a result of calculations to find out why Neptune's orbit was being disturbed by an unknown body.

WHAT MAKES NEPTUNE BLUE?

Neptune is covered with a blue ocean of liquid methane. It is a very cold place – at the furthest part of its orbit it is 4,000 million km (2,485 million miles) from the Sun. Its surface temperature drops to –210°C (–346°F). Neptune is made of hydrogen, helium, and methane, and probably has a rocky core. It takes an amazing 164.8 years to travel just once around the Sun. Neptune was first identified in 1846 when astronomers found that an unidentified planet was disturbing the orbit of Uranus.

?

DID YOU KNOW THAT NEPTUNE HAS HUGE STORMS? ONE OF THESE, THE GREAT DARK SPOT, COVERED AN AREA LARGER THAN THAT OF EARTH.

• FACT FILE •

Mars reaches a low of around –153 °C (–225°F) at the poles, and has small polar ice-caps that grow larger during the Martian winter.

WHAT IS THE KUIPER BELT?

An astronomer named Gerard Kuiper suggested that beyond Neptune lay a belt of celestial bodies made up from rock and ice. Astronomers now think that there may be as many as 100,000 large, comet-like objects in the Kuiper Belt, including the planet Pluto. The icy bodies in the Kuiper Belt are called minor members, or 'Plutinos' because they act like little Plutos and are very difficult to spot from Earth, even with the most powerful telescopes.

IF ALL THE OBJECTS IN THE KUIPER BELT JOINED TOGETHER, THEY WOULD FORM A PLANET THE SIZE OF EARTH.

• FACT FILE •

An object in space will be pulled into a spherical shape if its gravitational force is powerful enough. Because the objects in the Kuiper Belt do not have powerful gravitational pulls, they come in all sorts of shapes and sizes.

WHERE IS CALLISTO?

Callisto is a moon of Jupiter, which is bigger than the dwarf planet Pluto and almost as large as Mercury. It is one of the most heavily cratered bodies in the Solar System. Its surface is covered with craters of all sizes caused by the impact of asteroids and comets.

More than 4 billion years of bombardment have darkened Callisto's icy surface. The biggest impacts cracked the surface to form huge bull's-eye patterns. The surface is blanketed by dark dirt that accumulated when icy crater rims and cliffs crumbled away.

This satellite has a carbon dioxide atmosphere that is only slightly denser than the near-vacuum of outer space.

?

DID YOU KNOW THAT JUPITER HAS FOUR MOONS? IN SIZE ORDER THEY ARE GANYMEDE, CALLISTO, IO AND EUROPA.

• FACT FILE •

Callisto's diameter measures 4,806 km (2,986 miles). It orbits Jupiter every 16.7 days at a distance of 1,883,000 km (1,170,000 miles). It was discovered by Galileo in 1610.

WHERE IS THERE A MOON OF ICE?

Europa is a large moon of Jupiter. Its surface is made of ice, which may have an ocean of water beneath it. Such an ocean could provide a home for living things. The surface layer of ice or ice and water is 80 to 160km (50 to 100 miles) deep. The satellite has an extremely thin atmosphere.

Europa is one of the smoothest bodies in the Solar System. Its surface features include shallow cracks, valleys, ridges, pits, blisters and icy flows. None of them extend more than a few hundred metres upwards or downwards. In some places, huge sections of the surface have split apart and separated.

The surface of Europa has few impact craters. The splitting and shifting of the surface and disruptions from below have destroyed most of the old craters.

• FACT FILE •

Europa's interior is hotter than its surface. This internal heat comes from the gravitational forces of Jupiter and Jupiter's other large satellites, which pull Europa's interior in different directions.

ELECTRICALLY CHARGED PARTICLES FROM JUPITER'S RADIATION BELTS CONTINUOUSLY BOMBARD EUROPA'S SURFACE.

WHICH DWARF PLANET IS ALWAYS DARK AND COLD?

On Pluto it is always dark and cold, even in the middle of the day. This is because the Sun appears 1,000 times fainter from the surface of Pluto than it does from Earth, making it little more than a faint star.

In summer, Pluto has a slight atmosphere because the surface warms up sufficiently to melt some of its ice, turning it to gas. As Pluto moves away from the Sun, the gas freezes and becomes ice once more. This means that in winter, Pluto's weather doesn't just become worse, it disappears altogether.

• FACT FILE •

Little is known about Pluto's atmosphere, but it probably consists primarily of nitrogen with some carbon monoxide and methane.

WHICH IS PLUTO'S COMPANION MOON?

In 2009, scientists redefined the meaning of the word planet and Pluto was officially downgraded to the status of a dwarf planet: one of 44 rather than one of nine. Controversy reigns about this decision, and it does not prevent Pluto from being as fascinating a subject for study today, as it was in 1978, when the then planet was found to have a companion moon which scientists named Charon. The moon is one-third the size of Pluto making it the biggest, in comparison to its parent, in the entire Solar System. They are 20,000km (12,430 miles) apart.

In 2006, NASA launched the New Horizons probe to make a flyby study of Pluto and its moons. The probe reached its destination in 2015, sending amazing photos back to Earth.

• FACT FILE •

Pluto takes 248 years to orbit the Sun. Amazingly, this means that not even half a year has elapsed on this dwarf planet since its discovery in 1930! Another strange feature about Pluto is that it rotates in the opposite direction from most of the other planets.

WHAT IS A PLANETARY SATELLITE?

A satellite is a natural or artificial object that revolves around a larger astronomical object, usually a planet. Our Moon is the most obvious example. All the planets in the Solar System except Mercury and Venus have natural satellites. More than 60 such objects have so far been discovered. Saturn has the most satellites, with 18 certain and several more yet to be confirmed. The natural satellites vary greatly in size. Some of them measure only several kilometres in diameter, as in the case of the two tiny moons of Mars and the outer satellites of Jupiter.

• FACT FILE •

Ganymede is the largest satellite of Jupiter. It was discovered by the Italian astronomer Galileo Galilei in 1610 and named by the German astronomer Simon Marius after a figure in Greek mythology.

MERCURY AND VENUS ARE THE ONLY TWO PLANETS IN THE SOLAR SYSTEM THAT DO NOT HAVE ANY MOONS.

HOW COULD PLANETS COLLIDE?

Look up into the sky and see all the stars and planets and you might wonder if there might be a collision some day. But luckily this is not likely to happen. What we fail to realize is how much further away certain stars and planets are from the Earth than others. To get a better idea of this, let's consider our Solar System and its planets.

Let's imagine your head is the Sun in both size and location in the Solar System. Your head is then in the centre of a number of rings of different sizes. These rings are the orbits which the planets travel around the Sun. With your head as the centre, Mercury is the nearest (about 6m/20ft away from you), Venus moves around in the second ring (12m/40ft away), in the third ring is Earth (16m/52ft from your head), in the fourth ring is Mars, smaller than Earth, and 25m (82ft) away. Next is Jupiter, the largest of all the planets, in the sixth ring is Saturn, nearly a city street away, Uranus is nearly two streets away and finally, Pluto, which is nearly four streets away.

Since each of them goes around you in its orbit without ever changing, you can now see why they are not likely to bump into one another!

• FACT FILE •

The first person to travel in space was a Russian cosmonaut named Yuri Alekseyevich Gagarin. His spaceship was called *Vostok I* and he went on 12 April 1961.

WHY IS THERE NO LIFE ON THE OTHER PLANETS?

As far as we know, there is no form of life on any of the other planets in the Solar System.

It was assumed that light, water and oxygen – as seen at the Earth's surface – were necessary to life and we know that none of the other planets have these surface conditions. However, in the last few years it has been found that some life-forms need neither light nor oxygen as they live in a system that depends on sulphur from deep undersea volcanoes in conditions of extreme heat and pressure. So some scientists hope that life-forms might exist in similar extreme conditions elsewhere in the Solar System. Other possiblities that are being explored (or may be explored in the future) include Saturn's satellite Titan and Jupiter's satellite Europa, as well as several comets to see if they contain the basic materials to support life.

• FACT FILE •

Many asteroids have struck the Earth already, and many scientists believe that such an impact resulted in the extinction of the dinosaurs about 65 million years ago.

WHAT IS A BLACK HOLE?

Black holes are the monsters of the Universe. Formed from the brightest of all explosions, supernovae, they soon become the darkest objects in space, emitting no light at all.

A black hole is an area in space where the force of gravity is so strong that even light cannot escape from it. Black holes are created when a burned-out star collapses. Eventually it shrinks into a tiny sphere of material. The gravity of this material is so powerful that it pulls in everything around it. Even light itself is sucked into the black hole. Nothing that goes into a black hole ever comes out. We cannot see black holes.

• FACT FILE •

Imagine space as a stretched-out sheet. If an object is placed on this sheet, it will create a dip, towards which other objects will be drawn if they come too close. A black hole creates such a steep dip that objects that enter can never escape.

WHERE DO ASTEROIDS COME FROM?

An asteroid is any of numerous small planetary bodies that revolve around the Sun. Asteroids are also called minor planets or planetoids. Most of them are located in the asteroid belt between the orbits of Mars and Jupiter. The belt contains more than 1,150 asteroids with diameters greater than 30km (18 miles). Astronomers are not sure how the asteroids originated. According to the leading theory, however, most known asteroids are the shattered remains of a smaller group of larger objects.

It is believed that asteroids come from objects that were left over from the time the planets formed.

• FACT FILE •

Most asteroids drift harmlessly in their orbits around the Sun for billions of years. Occasionally, however, an asteroid may be knocked out of its orbit and sent on a collision course with a planet.

WHERE IS THERE A GIANT BALL OF GAS?

THERE ARE FOUR GAS GIANTS IN ALL. THEY ARE JUPITER, SATURN, URANUS AND NEPTUNE.

• FACT FILE •

The force of gravity at the surface of Jupiter is up to 2.4 times stronger than on Earth. So, an object that weighs 45kg (100lb) on Earth would weigh 108kg (240lb) on Jupiter.

Jupiter, the largest planet in the Solar System, is a giant ball of gas and liquid with little, if any, solid surface. Its diameter is 142,984km (88,846 miles), more than 11 times that of Earth, and about one-tenth that of the Sun. The planet's surface is composed of dense red, brown and white clouds.

In 1995 the *Galileo* probe dropped a smaller probe into the turbulent atmosphere of the gas giant. It took measurements for 57 minutes before it was destroyed by Jupiter's atmospheric pressure.

WHERE IS THE HUBBLE SPACE TELESCOPE IN ORBIT?

The Hubble Space Telescope is a powerful telescope orbiting 610km (380 miles) above the Earth. It is a reflecting telescope with a light-gathering mirror 240cm (94in) in diameter and provides sharper images of heavenly bodies than any other space telescope.

This is because the Hubble Space Telescope views the heavens without looking through the Earth's atmosphere. The atmosphere bends light due to a phenomenon known as diffraction, and the atmosphere is constantly moving. This combination of diffraction and movement causes starlight to jiggle about as it passes through the air, and so stars appear to twinkle.

THE HUBBLE TELESCOPE IS NAMED AFTER AMERICAN ASTRONOMER EDWIN P. HUBBLE, WHO MADE IMPORTANT CONTRIBUTIONS TO ASTRONOMY IN THE 1920S.

• FACT FILE •

Radio observatories have radio telescopes for the study of radio waves. Most radio telescopes use large antennae to capture radio waves from space. In most cases, computers guide the telescopes and analyze the data they collect.

WHERE WAS THE FIRST COMET IMPACT OBSERVED?

The space shuttle *Discovery* launched the Hubble Space Telescope into orbit in 1990. Soon after launch, engineers discovered a flaw in the telescope's light-gathering mirror. The flaw made the images less clear than they otherwise would have been. Engineers designed an optical device to bend light reflected by the mirror in a way that would make up for the error. Astronauts from the space shuttle *Endeavour* installed the device on the telescope in 1993, and it worked as planned.

Along with many other telescopes, the Hubble Space Telescope observed the bombardment of Jupiter by fragments of comet Shoemaker-Levy 9 in 1994. The images showed astonishing holes in Jupiter's atmosphere where the comet pieces smashed through. This bombardment was the first comet impact ever observed as it happened.

• FACT FILE •

The *Viking* probe visited Mars in 1976 in search of life. They conducted numerous tests on Martian soils but found no evidence of any living organisms.

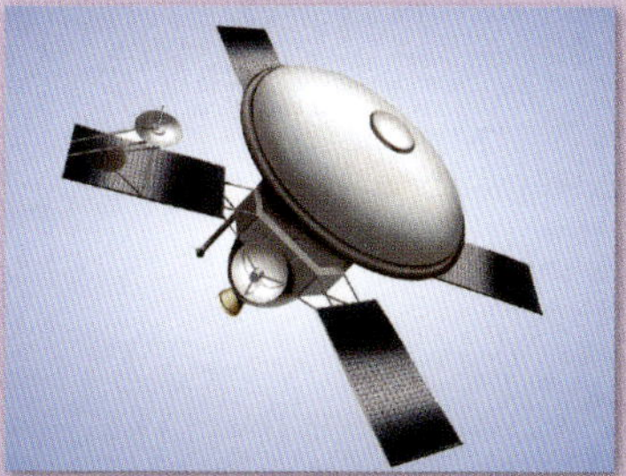

WHERE DO WE SEE METEOR SHOWERS?

The Earth meets a number of trails or clusters of tiny meteoroids at certain times every year. At such times, the sky seems filled with a shower of sparks. Streams and swarms have orbits like those of comets and are believed to be fragments of comets.

The most brilliant meteor shower known took place on 12–13 November 1833. It was one of the Leonid showers, which occur every November and seem to come from the direction of the constellation Leo.

? **DID YOU KNOW THAT METEORS THAT REACH THE GROUND ARE CALLED METEORITES?**

• FACT FILE •

Barringer Crater is a huge depression in the Earth in north-central Arizona. It measures about 1,275m (4,180ft) wide and 175m (570ft) deep. It was formed about 50,000 years ago when a meteorite struck the Earth.

WHAT ARE MAGELLANIC CLOUDS?

Magellanic Clouds are two galaxies visible in the Southern Hemisphere as small, hazy patches of light. They are the galaxies closest to the Milky Way, the galaxy that contains the Sun, the Earth and the rest of our Solar System. Astronomers classify the Magellanic Clouds as irregular galaxies because the distribution of the stars within them does not follow a particular pattern.

The Magellanic Clouds contain billions of stars, but individual stars can be distinguished only by using the most powerful telescopes. As a result, the galaxies appear cloudy to the naked eye. The Magellanic Clouds also contain a huge quantity of gas. New stars are constantly forming from this gas, which is composed mainly of hydrogen.

• FACT FILE •

Magellanic Clouds were first recorded in the early 16th century during the world's first circumnavigation by the Portuguese explorer Ferdinand Magellan, after whom they were named.

WHAT IS A SOLAR WIND?

Charged particles are constantly being given off by the Sun. They are known as the Solar Wind and are strongest when the sunspot activity is at its height. When the Solar Wind reaches the Earth's magnetic field, the charged particles interact with gases in the Earth's atmosphere 10km (6 miles) above the surface.

This interaction causes the particles to send out light, which is seen from Earth as an amazing lightshow, best visible from within the Arctic and Antarctic Circles. In the Northern Hemisphere this is known as the aurora borealis, and in the Southern Hemisphere as the aurora australis.

• FACT FILE •

Darker areas on the surface of the Sun are called sunspots. These areas of cooler gas occur when the Sun's magnetic field blocks the flow of heat from the core.

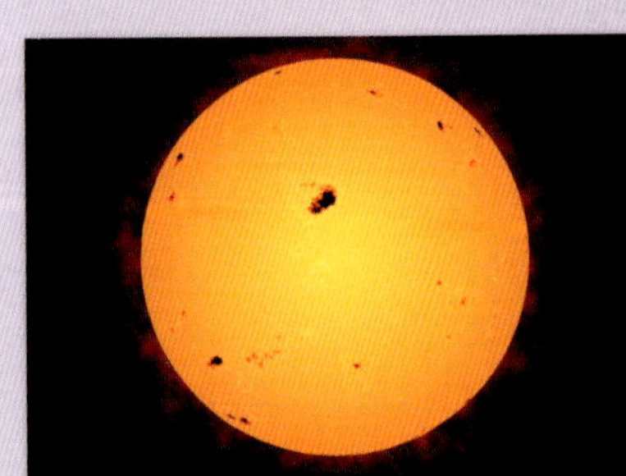

WHERE WOULD YOU SEE BAILEY'S BEADS?

A total eclipse of the Sun can be quite frightening, turning day into night in a spectacular fashion. However, as the Moon appears to eat the Sun, some incredibly beautiful 'special effects' take place. Just before the Sun disappears, a brilliant bright spot can be seen on the edge of the Moon, a little like a diamond on a ring. This is caused by the last fingers of the Sun's light filtering through valleys and mountain ranges on the Moon. Sometimes the bright spot can appear as an arc of glowing pearls, an effect known as Bailey's Beads.

FACT FILE

It is important never to look directly at the Sun, even during an eclipse. This can cause blindness.

Bailey's Beads take their name from Francis Baily (1774-1844), the English astronomer who was the first to describe them.

WHAT IS A DIFFUSE NEBULA?

Nebulae, which are clouds of dust and gas, come in many different shapes and sizes. Diffuse nebulae are extremely large structures, often many light-years wide, that have no definite outline and a sketchy, cloud-like appearance. They are either luminous or dark.

Diffuse nebulae shine as a result of the light of adjacent stars. They include some of the most striking objects in the sky, such as the Great Nebula in Orion. There are known to be many thousands of luminous nebulae in our Solar System.

DARK NEBULAE APPEAR SO BECAUSE THERE ARE NO NEARBY STARS TO LIGHT THEM. THEY CAN BE SPOTTED BECAUSE THEY BLOT OUT THE LIGHT FROM MORE DISTANT STARS.

• FACT FILE •

The only diffuse nebula visible to the naked eye is the beautiful Orion Nebula.

WHAT IS A STAR?

• FACT FILE •

As stars go, our Sun is very small. It is of a type known as a yellow dwarf. The colour of a star shows its surface temperature: red stars are relatively cool, while blue stars are hotter.

Stars are huge balls of burning gas that are scattered throughout the Universe. They burn for millions of years, giving off both light and heat. Stars produce energy by a process called nuclear fusion. The coolest stars are red and dim, while the hottest stars give off blue-white light. The temperatures on their surface range from 3,500°C (6,332°F) for cooler stars to over 40,000°C (72,000°F) for the hottest stars.

A new star is born when gas and dust are drawn together by gravity, forming a huge clump. It heats up until nuclear fusion begins, and the new star appears in the sky.

WHAT IS A SUPERNOVA?

The Milky Way only has around two supernovae per century, but they are very difficult to spot.

Sometimes a star appears in the sky quite suddenly. This happens when there is a pair of stars rotating together. These are called binaries, and there is usually one large star called a red giant, orbiting with a smaller, hotter star. The nova takes place when gas is drawn from the red giant into the smaller star, where the heat causes a massive explosion and emits huge amounts of light. A supernova takes place when a star collapses as it begins to burn out, then suddenly explodes, producing a huge amount of light energy, and leaving behind a tiny core of neutrons, which is the heaviest substance in the Universe.

• FACT FILE •

Even with today's most powerful and advanced equipment, there is no visible limit to the Universe. No one is totally sure of the shape of the Universe.

WHAT IS THE TAIL OF A COMET?

Comets are sometimes known as 'cosmic' or 'dirty' snowballs.

You cannot see the nucleus of a comet with the naked eye, but you can sometimes see its tail. It appears as a smear of light that moves very gradually across the sky. As a comet moves closer to the Sun, the ice and other frozen gases in its nucleus begin to boil off, producing a long tail of gas and dust. The tail will always point away from the Sun because light and other forms of radiation from the Sun push against the minute particles present within the tail.

Comet tails can be very different in shape and size. Some are short and stubby, while others are long and slender. As the tail grows, the comet gains in speed because it is nearing the Sun.

• FACT FILE •

Halley's Comet is perhaps the most famous comet of all. It can be seen from Earth every 76 years and was even recorded in 1066 on the Bayeux Tapestry.

WHERE IS NASA LOCATED?

DID YOU KNOW THAT THE INTERNATIONAL SPACE STATION COULD FLY TO THE MOON AND BACK IN A DAY? IT REACHES SPEEDS OF 7.71 KM/S (4.791 MILES PER SECOND).

The National Aeronautics and Space Administration (NASA) is located on Merritt Island, across from a point of land called Cape Canaveral in Florida, USA. People often call it Cape Canaveral because it was formerly located there.

NASA tests, repairs and launches space shuttles at Kennedy Space Center. To prepare a shuttle for launch, workers in the 52-storey Vehicle Assembly Building attach the external fuel tank to the orbiter (the craft that carries the crew) and two booster rockets. A huge tractor-like machine called a crawler then carries the shuttle to one of two launch pads.

• FACT FILE •

With the help of robots and special equipment, astronauts are able to carry out difficult repairs on satellites and space stations.

WHAT IS A SPACE STATION?

Space stations allow the crew to work in space for long periods in conditions of zero gravity. While conditions in space capsules and the space shuttle are cramped, space stations are more suitable for longer stays in space. Rockets or the space shuttle bring supplies of air and food to the space station, and often a replacement crew. Space stations are constructed from modules that are small enough to be carried by rockets or the space shuttle, which are assembled once they are in orbit.

• FACT FILE •

Skylab was the first US space station. One of its tasks was to test how humans behaved in microgravity.

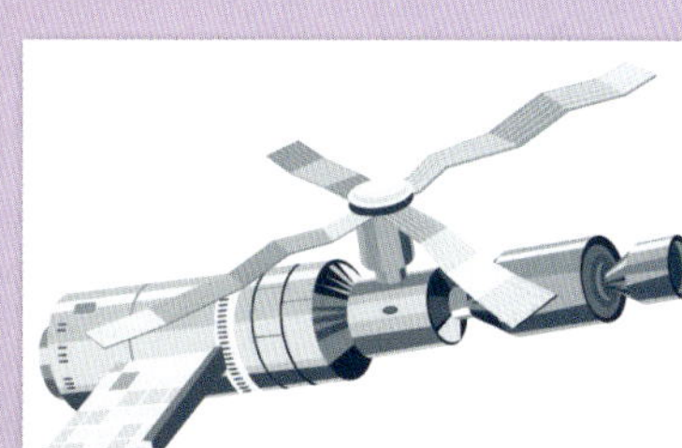

WHAT ARE SPACESUITS MADE OF?

Spacesuits are made of specially adapted man-made materials, for example, urethane-coated nylon. Designing a spacesuit is a very complex procedure, as the spacesuit needs to give the astronaut complete control and protection; in fact, it needs to act like a miniature spacecraft. It provides everything that an astronaut requires to survive for short periods in space, including oxygen to breathe, water to drink, heating and cooling devices, communication apparatus and toilet facilities. These suits have been developed to withstand the extreme conditions of space.

SPACESUITS CONTAIN POUCHES FOR STORING WATER AND URINE!

FACT FILE

The suit maintains a constant pressure by surrounding the body with a kind of balloon. This balloon is full of air, which presses against the body in the same way as the Earth's atmosphere.

WHERE DO ASTRONAUTS DO THEIR TRAINING?

NASA astronauts do their mission training in a variety of places, including in high-flying aircraft to learn how to cope with weightlessness, and in water tanks in the 'Neutral Buoyancy Facility' to learn how to move in their bulky space suits. Most of the facilities are at the Johnson Space Center in Houston, Texas.

Astronauts preparing to stay on the International Space Station also train at the Russian Yuri Gagarin Cosmonaut Training Centre (Star City) outside Moscow, which is named after the first human being in space.

• FACT FILE •

NASA has sophisticated simulators that can reproduce any aspect of a mission on a craft such as the Space Shuttle. Pilots can spend time learning how to manoeuvre the craft while others can learn how to operate the other instruments.

HOW DO ASTRONAUTS TRAVEL ON THE MOON'S SURFACE?

• FACT FILE •

Altogether there have been six Apollo missions to the Moon, during which 12 astronauts have explored its conditions and composition. They have tested the soil to determine what the Moon is made from and also measured moonquakes.

In later Apollo missions, astronauts took the Lunar Rover or Moon Buggy with them. This enabled them to explore further than had been possible before. Equipment on board the buggy included a television camera and a satellite dish so that pictures could be sent back to Earth. To avoid damage from the rough surface of the Moon, the tyres were solid. Steering was controlled by a small hand control rather than a wheel. The Lunar Rover was powered by a battery, and its top speed was just under 20km/h (12 mph). It also carried tool kits and bags for geological samples.

WHY WILL FOOTPRINTS STAY ON THE MOON FOREVER?

The footprints and buggy tracks left by Apollo astronauts will last for centuries because there is no wind on the Moon.

The Moon does not have any atmosphere, so there is no weather as we are used to on Earth. Because there is no atmosphere to trap heat, the temperatures on the Moon vary dramatically over the course of a day, from 100°C (212°F) at noon to –173°C (–279°F)at night. The Moon has no rain or earthquakes to wear away or break down the craters, so they have remained the same for millions of years.

The Moon does not produce its own light, but it looks bright because it reflects light from the Sun. Think of the Sun as a light bulb, and the Moon as a mirror, reflecting light from the light bulb. The lunar phase changes as the Moon orbits the Earth and different portions of its surface are illuminated by the Sun.

• FACT FILE •

Sometimes the Moon appears orange. This occurs when there is a lot of dust, smoke or pollution in the atmosphere. The size of those particles will determine what you see. Sometimes it looks red, orange ... even blue.

THE FLAG THE AMERICANS LEFT ON THE MOON IS HELD OUT BY A METAL BAR BECAUSE THERE IS NO WIND TO MAKE IT FLY.

HOW DID WE BENEFIT FROM THE DISCOVERY OF INFRARED?

Infrared satellites have been used to monitor the Earth's weather, to study vegetation patterns, and to monitor geology and ocean temperatures.

Sir Frederick William Herschel (1738–1822) was born in Germany, and became well known both as a musician and an astronomer. His experiments with light proved to be important, not only because they led to the discovery of infrared, but also because it was the first time that someone showed there were forms of light not visible to us.

Today, infrared technology has many exciting and useful applications. In the field of infrared astronomy, new and fascinating discoveries are being made about the Universe. Medical infrared imaging is a very useful diagnostic tool. Infrared cameras are used for police and security work as well as in fire fighting and in the military. Infrared imaging is used to detect heat loss in buildings and in testing electronic systems.

• FACT FILE •

Ultraviolet and X-ray astronomy are radiation sources of a higher energy level than infrared and are best observed by telescopes orbiting Earth's atmosphere. Ultraviolet astronomy is used to track down the hottest stars.

HOW DOES SPACE RESEARCH HELP US IN DAILY LIFE?

Everyone has benefitted from the technology that was developed for use in space. Scientists not only study living organisms, but they can also study combustion in microgravity to help design more efficient jet engines. In addition, the study of crystal growth has helped us to build better semiconductors for computers.

Microchips that are used in everything from digital watches to computers were first developed so that lots of equipment could fit into a small spacecraft. Advances such as keyhole surgery, solar power and many ordinary household items such as Velcro and kitchen foil have come about because of science from space technology.

• FACT FILE •

Professional astronomers today hardly ever use telescopes. Instead, a telescope sends an object's light to a photographic plate or to an electronic light-sensitive computer chip called a charge-coupled device, or CCD. CCDs are about 50 times more sensitive than film, so today's astronomers can record in a minute an image that would have taken about an hour to record on film.

WHICH IS THE LARGEST TELESCOPE IN THE WORLD?

Two identical telescopes called Keck I and Keck II are the largest reflecting telescopes in the world. Each has a segmented mirror 10m (33ft) in diameter. The telescopes are on Mauna Kea, a mountain in Hawaii.

The telescope is in an optical observatory that stands under a large dome with shutters. The dome and the shutters protect the telescope from the weather. Motors and precision gears keep the telescope pointed in the desired direction as the Earth rotates. Observatories use two principal kinds of optical telescopes – reflecting telescopes and refracting telescopes. Reflecting telescopes use a set of such mirrors to focus light, and refracting telescopes use a system of lenses.

• FACT FILE •

Refracting telescopes need thick lenses for high magnification. The refracting telescope at the Yerkes Observatory in Williams Bay, Wisconsin, is the world's largest lens. It measures 102 cm (40 in) in diameter.

ARE THERE REALLY UFOS?

An unidentified flying object (or UFO) is a light or object in the air that has no obvious explanation. Some people believe UFOs are spaceships from other planets. However, investigators discover ordinary explanations for most UFO sightings, largely because most witnesses are generally reliable individuals. Many reported UFOs are actually bright planets, stars or meteors. People have reported aircraft, missiles, satellites, birds, swarms of insects and weather balloons as UFOs.

Investigators can explain all but a small percentage of UFO reports. The remainder may be due to an unknown phenomenon or to limitations in human perception and memory. Most scientists believe that there is not enough reliable evidence to connect these sightings with life from other planets.

Unusual weather conditions can also create optical illusions that are reported as UFOs.

FACT FILE

Some UFOs are called 'flying saucers'. This term was coined by the press in 1947 to describe a sighting by Kenneth Arnold, a civilian pilot, who reported unknown objects speeding through the air.

PICTURE CREDITS

Images supplied by Dreamstime

Icons: Earth (5, 6–33) Fourleaflover; chemistry flask (5, 34–51) Elena Dyachenko; molecule (5, 52–73) Kamigami; microphone (5, 74–95) Artizarus; gear (5, 96–129) Sunil Lal; rocket (5, 130–175) Pavel Strezhnev; Hand (throughout) Selman Amer.

10b Pixelrobot; 11t Lom6605; 11b Katatonia82; 14b Joshua Rainey; 15t Danmir12; 15b Piyathep; 16b Oxygen64; 18t Ali Nishan; 19t Joseph Gough; 19b Asist; 20t Maksim Loskutnikov; 20b Russell Shively; 21t Vismax; 21b Sergey Uryadnikov; 22b Brian Kushner; 23b Jiajianzheng; 24t Laurence Romaric; 24b Ali Ender Birer; 27b Erik Mandre; 28t Khunaspix; 28bl Ivan Kmit; 28br Dastin50; 29b Fredleonero; 31b Chris Fourie; 32b Nikita Zabellevitš; 36t Franz Pfluegl; 36b Sahua; page 37b, 42t, 45tl, 46t, 146b Georgios Kollidas; 38b Sebastian Kaulitzki; 39b Fabrizio Zanier; 40t Olha Rohulya; 41r skypixel; 41l Glazyuk; 41b Robyn Mackenzie; 42b Evgenyatamanenko; 43bl Thanamat; 44b Marian Vejcik; 44c Andesign101; 45br Dave Bredeson; 46b Ron Sumners; 47t Christopher Smith; 47b Promotive; 48c Kittichai Kasemsarn; 49t Pablo631; 49b Ivan Cholakov; 50b Isselee; 54t Jalfoto; 54b Larry Gevert; 54t Beata Becla; 54b Odrachenko; 56b Tomislav Forgo; 57t Nicky Linzey; 58b Szefei; 59t Carlos Caetano; 60tl Ignasi Martín; 60r Charlotte Leaper; 61t Stefano Lunardi; 61b Ken Cole; 62b Jan Kratochvila; 63t Hywit Dimyadi; 63b Empire331; 66t Atman; 67t Serg_velusceac; 68t Elena Butinova; 68b Serdar Başak; 69t Surachaikunprayot; 70t Pierre Landry; 71t Emily Horne; 71b Margo555; 72t Joseph Gough; 72b Les Cunliffe; 73t Wisconsinart; 73b Tihis; 77t Shawn Hempel; 78b Cristian andrei Matei; 79t Nik Frey; 81t Alessio Viviani; 81bl Photozirka; 81br Tupungato; 82t Mircea Dobre; 82b Jruffa; 83t Linqong; 83b Tamifreed; 84t Frogtravel; 84b Henrik Andersen; 85b Claudiodivizia; 86t, 87b Wangkun Jia; 86b Leonello Calvetti; 89t Typhoonski; 89br Alistair Scott; 90t Filosof77; 90b Roza; 91t Editor77; 91b Chrisstanley; 92t Mav888; 93t Philcold; 94t Pavelmidi1968; 94b Edwin Verin; 95t Photomyeye; 95b Xneo; 98b Brett Critchley; 100t Carlosphotos; 102b Sofiia Kravchenko; 103b Ljupco; 106b Yinan Zhang; 107t Roxana González; 107b Sergey Khakimullin; 108t Vladimirfloyd; 108b Fotoeye75; 109b Leonid Smirnov; 110t Rob Hill; 110b Pressureua; 111t Paul Jantz; 112b Embe2006; 113t Mikalai Bachkou; 113b Robert Chlopas; 114b Olesiaru; 116t Scanrail; 116b Pschenck; 117t Boarding1now; 118/119t Robert Adrian Hillman; 118b Robert Paul Van Beets; 119c Alexan24; 119b Elena Elisseeva; 120t Mike_kiev; 120b Bcbounders; 121t Andrey Armyagov; 121b Vladislav Gurfinkel; 122b Aivolie; 123t Andrew Barker; 123b Duncan Noakes; 124t Soundsnaps; 124b Scanrail; 125t Nils Ackermann; 125b PureSolution; 126tr Matthew Apps; 126bl Flynt; 128t Andrei Malov; 128b Kts; 129t Mishoo; 129c Dmyla; 129b Arkadi Bojaršinov; 132/133t Selestron76; 132b Amanda Lewis; 133b Thomas Jurkowski; 134t Alexandr Mitiuc; 134b Michal Bednarek; 135t Jut; 135b Mik3812345; 136t Jessamine; 137t Petrosg; 137b Janne Skinnarla; 138t Rfischia; 138b Clearviewstock; 139b Jiajianzheng; 139t Patryk Kosmider; 140t Orlando Florin Rosu; 140b Jankaliciak; 141t, 155t Maxcortesiphoto; 141b Elena Duvernay; 142t, 158t Mopic; 142b Dannyphoto80; 143t Maxcortesiphoto; 144t Aaron Rutten; 144b Designpicssub; 145t Paul Fleet; 145b, 149t Eugen Dobric; 146t, 150b, 167b Patrimonio Designs Limited; 147t Davidebner; 147b Christopher Ewing; 148t Forplayday; 150t Sergii Koval; 151t Diego Barucco; 151b Andrey Shevchenko; 152t Rolffimages; 152b Neverhood; 153t Rastan; 154t Sdecoret; 156t Nerthuz; 156b Alain Lacroix; 157t Les Cunliffe; 158b Walter Arce; 159t Yury Dmitrienko; 159b Ugchannel; 160t Roman Krochuk; 160b Olesiaru; 161b Cednik; 161b Mrotchua; 162t Solarseven; 162b, 168b Francesa; 163t Elena Schweitzer; 163b Dvmsimages. 164t Kevin Carden; 164b PixelParticle; 165t Solarseven; 165b Suyerry; 166t Edwin Verin; 166b Chris Galbraith; 167t Leonello Calvetti; 168t Edwin Verin; 169t, 169b Adrian Lindley; 170t Jdanne; 170b, 175t Luca Oleastri; 171t William Attard Mccarthy; 171b G. K.; 172t Suljo; 172b Oleksandr Umanets; 173t Empire331; 173b Sergii Shcherbakov; 174tl Kelpfish; 175b Appler.